PROBLEMS AND PERSPECTIVES IN RELIGIOUS DISCOURSE

PROBLEMS AND PERSPECTIVES IN RELIGIOUS DISCOURSE

Advaita Vedānta Implications

JOHN GRIMES

State University of New York Press

Published by
State University of New York Press, Albany

Printed in the United States of America

For information, address State University of New York Press,
State University Plaza, Albany, NY 12246

Production by Christine Lynch
Marketing by Theresa A. Swierzowski

Library of Congress Cataloging-in-Publication Data

Grimes, John, Ph. D.
Problems and perspectives in religious discourse : Advaita Vedānta implications / John Grimes.
p. cm.
Includes bibliographical references and index.
ISBN 0–7914–1791–3 (alk. paper). : ISBN 0–7914–1792–1 (pbk. : alk. paper)
1. Language and languages—Religious aspects. 2. Language and languages—Philosophy. 3. Advaita. 4. Vedanta. I. Title.
BL65.L2G76 1994 1994
200'.14—dc20 93–18516
CIP

10 9 8 7 6 5 4 3 2 1

CONTENTS

PREFACE

SPECIAL FEATURE OF THE WORK

The present work is an attempt to look at the problem(s) connected with religious discourse in a new light. It proposes a new solution to an ancient problem.[1] It delineates a way of bringing together the dilemma found inherent in religious declarations, both Eastern and Western, with one branch of Indian philosophy, that is, Advaita Vedānta. Its chief concern is to overcome the "gap" which has rendered religious discourse problematic.

Religious discourse attempts to point to, describe, and guide one to the "promised land"—whether that be God, the Absolute, heaven, happiness, peace, or however one wants to describe the "goal of life." Such an agenda renders religious statements frought with paradoxes and self-contradictions. Can what is claimed to be *inexpressible* ever be *expressed*? Is it possible to *believe in* that which appears to be inherently contradictory?

What do the words used in religious discourse *mean* and what *function*(s) do they have? Are they cognitive, factual, and verifiable, or are they noncognitive, non-factual, and unverifiable? This work posits and depicts two paradigmatic approaches to these questions. Either religious discourse refers to an "other" and the approach to this remote and foreign "other" must be through perception or mediated concepts, or, religious discourse refers to the very constitutive being of anything whatsoever and as such is self-evident, immediate, and certain.[2] This is not a false dilemma. Either the Divine is somehow totally different from oneself (*dvaita* or *bheda*), different-cum-non-different (*viśiṣṭādvaita* or *bhedabheda*) or non-different (*advaita*). And even among those systems who advocate non-duality, except for Advaita Vedānta, there is "some sort" of "otherness" posited.

The former approach postulates a gap between Divinity/God/Reality and the individual while the latter approach emphasizes absolute identity. Most, if not all of the proposed solutions to the problem of religious discourse, both of the West and of the East, fall under the approach to an "other." Advaita's solution declares that religious discourse primarily concerns individuals, here and now, and not a God, above and beyond. Methodologically its analysis commences with empirical *existence* and culminates in (trans-empirical) *essence,* declaring that in fact the two are not different. It refers to that which is immediately evident and immanently present[3] (*Ātman/Brahman*)—unlike the general approaches to an "other," which, in one degree or another, search "elsewhere."

REASONS THE THEME WAS CHOSEN

This theme was chosen for a number of reasons. The problem(s) of religious discourse has existed within philosophy for thousands of years and to this day there is no one definitive solution. In fact, the majority of solutions presented are not even viable possibilities,[4] being as they are contradictions and inconsistencies.[5] Merely because this topic has virtually "run its course" in current Western academic circles (as the topic of the day) does not in any way lesson this analysis. As far as my knowledge goes, no one has attempted to solve this problem of religious discourse from the perspective of Advaita Vedānta in a thorough manner.

Second, the problem of religious discourse has been a contemporary subject of enquiry, both within the disciplines of Philosophy and Religious Studies. Though the central issue of the debate has currently turned from the question of whether God's existence can be proven,[6] it still centers upon the elusive concept of "God" and oft times finds itself wrestling with the non-anthropomorphic Absolute or Ground of Being. In fact, the Absolute (in its non-dual aspect) has become a topic of some fascination in recent years.

Finally, this theme allows one to do philosophy with a religious theme. It is still almost a "voice in the wilderness" when the claim is put forward that Indian philosophy is philosophy (or can be presented as pure philosophy on anyone's definition of exactly what philosophy is) and not only, merely, exclusively theology.[7] Indian philosophy is still, in many instances, incorrectly taught in Western circles as something outlandish, sexually oriented, culturally degenerating, unrealistic, quietistic, illusionistic, and/or undesirable. Such teachers do not even suspect that Indian philosophy has an intellectual content.[8] Thus, this theme, gives scope for demonstrating how philosophical issues are as relevant to Indian philosophy as religious issues—East or West.

CONTRIBUTIONS OF THE WORK

The uniqueness of this work and its contributions to philosophy/religious studies are three-fold. First, this thesis proposes that all religious discourse can be interpreted not only as cognitive, but also as valid. This in itself is not a unique claim, but it becomes so when Advaita adds that since the referent of religious discourse is immediately present as the constitutive being of everything whatsoever, and therefore is self-evident and certain, it is fundamental and prior to all proofs which must presuppose it. Yet, it does not presuppose itself as it is the one indubitable fact of experience which can never be denied without self-contradiction. Flew's challenge of falsifiability is met at the empirical (*vyāvahārika*) level (wherein, according to Advaita, ignorance (*avidyā*) holds court). But actually, and here is the real uniqueness of Advaita, *all* language *directly* and *cognitively* asserts the Reality. "Those who have eyes can see; those who have ears can hear."

Dharmarāja was one of the few Advaitins to claim that the Great Sayings (*mahāvākya*) *directly* posit identity. The general trend was to resort to secondary implication (*lakṣaṇa*). By attributing a two-level theory of religious discourse at the empirical level, this work explores and explicates a possible expansion to Dharmarāja's contention and proposes a second contribution. This proposition is that: There is a first level of language which is a literal expression directly naming the fact of the non-dual Absolute, and there is a second level of language, which is secondary, indirect, symbolic, and figurative.

The third contribution of this work is that, contrary to common belief, it is more logically consistent to speak of the unqualified Absolute than of a theistic deity. The general idea is that an anthropomorphic God is comprehensible (emotionally satisfying, loving, etc.) but inappropriate as an object of worship and that a non-anthropomorphic God is utterly incomprehensible. An attempt is made to ground the incomprehensible Absolute within each one's own personal experience thus making it more than a mere assertion or theoretical concept and establishing it as an indubitable fact of experience.

ACKNOWLEDGMENTS

The present work is a substantially revised version of my doctoral thesis, originally submitted and accepted for the Ph.D. degree of the Radhakrishnan Institute for Advanced Study in Philosophy, University of Madras. I would like to express my deepest gratitude to Professor R. Balasubramanian, past-Director of the RIASP and mentor who taught, inspired, and encouraged me to dive deep into the Indic ocean. I owe an equal debt to Professor P. K. Sundaram of the RIASP for suggesting that I take up this subject, one which interested him deeply. Day after day I would approach him with questions and seek solutions to each particular philosophical problem I encountered. These two professors were my first formal/scholastic Advaita Vedānta *gurus*. I thank Professor K. S. Satchidananda Murty of Andhra University, Waltair for his query: "Do you mean to say that you are proposing that it is more logically consistent to speak of the unqualified Absolute than of a theistic deity?" His keen insight and clear, concise summation opened vistas which months of research had not so illumined. I am thankful also to Professor Ninian Smart, for his continued guidance, critiques, and support. My gratitude goes to Charlene Sawatsky for typing the manuscript. I thank the University of Madras and the University of Lethbridge, Alberta, Canada for providing me with the opportunities to write and refine this work. I offer my *pranāms* to the SYDA Foundation for providing me with the wherewithall to complete the work.

I must thank all the reviewers of this work who suggested/demanded/implored me to write and re-write again and again. Though everyone may still not be satisfied, its evolution has been gratifying.

I would like to thank the State University of New York Press and William Eastman for their assistance. Bill has made my life enriched beyond description.

Finally, to Meera, I owe a debt beyond repayment. Without her *śakti* blazing forth, the very opportunity to even commence this project would not have seen the light of day. She alone knows how true that is.

JOHN GRIMES
January, 1993

CHAPTER 1

Introduction

> I ask as a fool who knows not his own spirit:
> Where are the hidden traces left by the Gods?
> *Ṛg Veda* 1, 164, 5

THE WORLD[1] OF ADVAITA VEDĀNTA

Again and again one hears Advaita proclaim the necessity, and greatness, of "enquiry" (*viveka*). In order to begin to have an insight into the Indian philosophical system known as Advaita Vedānta, it appears one must question one's most cherished presuppositions, that is: Was I born? Am I my physical body? Am I my thoughts? Am I really so and so? How do I know that I exist? Who were my parents? Have they created me or have I created them? Who am I?

How does one know that one is reading a book right now? This is not a rhetorical question. (We all learned such knowledge at our mother's knee.) We can see the book, smell it, touch it, taste it, even hear it (if we drop the book). Everyone believes that this is something we can "take to the bank." It is sure and certain. The five senses are our bedrock touchstones. And of the five, sight is primary. For, don't we often say, "oh, I see!," to convey correct understanding, comprehension.

However, suppose one were to go outside and *watch* the sun traverse the sky on a clear day. What is wrong with this picture? We all know that the sun *does not* move. Yet we *see* it. Suppose one were to stand on a railroad track and peer down the tracks. What would one see? The tracks *appear* to come together at some distant point. Yet we all know that one could walk forever down those tracks and they would *never* merge together. Suppose one were to hold a stick under water. We would see that the stick is bent. Yet we all know that the stick is not really bent. These examples could be multiplied on end. The point is, our senses (or, more accurately, our mental interpretations) have betrayed us. And what can betray us in one instance, may do so in another. Is there any water in a mirage? Will there ever be any water in a mirage? And yet, inexplicably, wonderously, we perceive this "non-existent water." A non-existent dream-lion chases one in a dream and, as the lion plunges at one's throat, the dreamer awakens with a jolt to discover a beating heart and sweat on the forehead. A seemingly non-existent, illusory entity producing real results. How strange!

Because one believes in oneself, the thinker, the seer, the hearer, and so forth, one has faith that what one thinks, sees, and hears is (take it to the bank) "REAL." Instead, why not doubt the things which come and go, for example, thoughts, sights, sounds, and hold onto that which is always there and is foundational to it all—yourself.[2] The "I AM" can never be changed into "I AM NOT." What is experienced is always open to doubt. The *meaning* of what is experienced can always be doubted. But, that *someone* experienced is certain.

Language may be very misleading. One may assume, perhaps unconsciously, that reality is approachable through knowledge (*vidyā*), through thoughts, through information. Then, logically, one quite naturally assumes that there must also exist a knower of reality beyond the knowledge, beyond the thoughts, beyond the information known. But, the question may be asked, can Reality be known? Knowledge, as well as ignorance, may be of the mind only. Let us investigate.

To enquire into the purport of Advaita Vedānta is to enquire into an insight in search of What-Is. It is to quest after what is Real, what is Ultimate, what is of lasting value, certainty. In this day and age, every Western television-movie viewer knows that the "final frontier" is space. But space is not the *final* frontier. The final frontier carries with it an odor of finality, of completeness, of certainty. No matter how far one travels outwardly, Advaita avers that the final frontier will always be within. One may always doubt whatever one encounters as an "other." One could travel to heaven and look over to the throne of God and wonder whether that "entity" over there is really God or not. One may always doubt the "other." We are smart enough, sophisticated enough, to know about dreams and hallucinations and visions and illusions and relative perspectives. Think about it—all one may be certain of right now is that one is present. This book may not be real, the act of reading may not be real, but that *you* are present is indubitable.

Is there something certain, something that one may *never* doubt. Advaita avers one can never doubt one's own Self, the doubter him or herself. No matter where one finds oneself, oneself is *always* there. Why, the very act of doubting oneself is but an affirmation of oneself, for, one can always ask, "who exactly is doing the doubting?" To say that "I do not exist" is to affirm the "I" who is doing the doubting.

Who is this "I"? That is the essence of Advaita and, according to Advaita, the essence of all language—religious or otherwise. But I am getting ahead of myself.

THE PROBLEM

Ordinary language is quite messy, very problematic.[3] Why is there a special problem concerning specifically religious discourse? Religious discourse attempts to point to, analyze, describe, guide one to the "promised land." This renders religious discourse full of paradoxes and contradictions. For instance, traditional statements claim that God is incorporeal or, that God is a spirit. Thus, what does it mean to say: "The arm of the Lord is sure, the eye of the Lord is steadfast; God is a jealous and angry God"? How can one say that God is physically indescribable without indicating somehow *what it is* that is being said to be indescribable? It would appear that religious assertions are not genuine assertions at all but a kind of "double-think."

In both Eastern and Western philosophies/religions, the status of religious discourse has been critiqued in various ways. Distinctions can be discerned and described along lines of description, meaning, interpretation, apprehension, expression, convention, and contrasting perspectives. The sum result of this scholarship is that the very possibility of a philosophical understanding of religious discourse has been called into question.[4] The purpose of this book is an attempt to show that, because of its *radically* unique metaphysical standpoint,[5] Advaita Vedānta's use and understanding of religious statements is not subject to these common criticisms which are leveled against other systems. Advaita, it is true, may be subject to *other* criticisms. It is my claim that incoherence and self-contradiction is not one of them.

The aim of this book is to examine the main concepts, and especially the purport, of the philosophy of Advaita Vedānta vis-à-vis religious knowledge. It goes without saying that this unavoidably requires a certain arbitrariness. This is not to say that the historical development of Advaita is unimportant. It is not to say that I will focus on one particular individual Advaita exponent or try to give an overall historical development of the school. This is for two reasons. First and foremost, I am trying to present an insight into "how' the philosophical idea known as "advaita" would encompass the problem of religious knowledge. Second, the problem of the historical analysis of Advaita is not as straightforward and simple as might seem at first sight.

In recent times, there have been numerous attempts to interpret the history of Advaita Vedānta, especially the thought of Śaṅkara. T. M. P. Mahadevan posits that Advaitins knew of Buddhist thought and any similarities in presentation, vocabulary, or doctrine were simply tactical devices for overcoming their opponents. Some attempted to divide Śaṅkara's work into several stages, that is, pre, early, middle, and late.[6] Others believed that Śaṅkara's thought coincides with Buddhism, especially Mahāyāna Buddhism.[7] And still others[8] propose that the differences between early Advaitins and Buddhists were "largely a matter of emphasis and background rather than one of real essence."[9]

Some scholars may aver that Advaita Vedānta is not a single, uniform system of thought. I am well aware of the fact that Advaita is usually divided into pre-Śaṅkara, Śaṅkara, and post-Śaṅkara positions as well as the fact that Advaita has two major "ways" (*prasthāna*) or "school": The *Bhāmatī-prasthāna* and the *Vivaraṇa-prasthāna*, with their many adherents presenting subtle and not so subtle differences in doctrine. As well, there are post-Śaṅkara Advaitains who do not fit neatly into either school.

However, it must be stressed that these differences are only *exegetical* and not doctrinal. These differences have arisen in the course of the elucidation of a particular point of view, in the clarification of an issue, in the answering of an objection and so on. All such differences take place only within the framework of Advaita Vedānta. Every perspective, every mode of interpretation, which are each no doubt significant and insightful, are relative and are intended only to help one realize the *inward Self*.[10] Such differences are not irreconcilable within the framework of Advaita nor do they make Pre-Śaṅkara Advaita, Śaṅkara's Advaita, and post-Śaṅkara Advaita a house divided against itself.

It is precisely because of the central theme of Advaita, that is, the identity of *ātman* and *Brahman*, that the two separate though related problems regarding the meaningfulness of religious knowledge are resolved. The first dilemma: does language function differently when it is used to make religious statements and, second, how is one to distinguish true from false religious statements?

It is an acknowledged fact, even by the Western proponents who advocated their various solutions,[11] that the existent proposed solutions to the problem(s) inherent in religious discourse are full of self-contradictions—even *if* one is to grant their presuppositions. This is a crucial point—even *if* one is to grant their presuppositions. It is my claim that if one is to grant Advaita's presuppositions, then what follows is logically consistent and coherent.[12]

TWO ASSERTIONS

It is true that this work includes a short review of the basic epistemological and metaphysical positions propounded by Advaita Vedānta. However, the purpose behind presenting these viewpoints is to provide a background against, and out of which, a radical Advaitic theory of religious discourse will emerge. More than an apologetic, this work is intended to state two radically new assertions in regards to theories of religious discourse.[13]

These two assertions are:

1. Religious discourse can be interpreted to be not only cognitive, but also valid.

This in itself is not a unique claim, but it becomes so when Advaita adds to it that since the referent of religious discourse is immediately present as the constitutive being of everything whatsoever, and therefore self-evident and certain, it is fundamental and prior to all proofs which must necessarily presuppose it. Yet it does not presuppose itself as it is the one indubitable fact of experience, which can never be denied without self-contradiction. Advaita's vision claims that for the qualified aspirant, religious discourse directly and cognitively asserts the Reality and that for the non-qualified aspirant, religious discourse indirectly, or, in specific cases, directly asserts the Absolute. And . . .

2. Contrary to common belief, it is more philosophically and logically consistent to speak of the unqualified Absolute than of a theistic deity.[14]

The general idea is that an anthropomorphic God is comprehensible but inappropriate as an object of worship and that a non-anthropomorphic God is utterly incomprehensible. An attempt is made to ground the incomprehensible Absolute within each one's own personal experience thus making it more than a mere assertion or theoretical concept and establishing it as an indubitable fact of experience.

RELIGION AND LANGUAGE

It is remarkable that one is able to make a meaningful statement about an entity who or which is alleged, by the very person making the statement, to be transcendent to the finite world and radically different from it. Thus, it is that religious discourse raises an interesting and intriguing problem. Its subject matter involves a reality which is trans-human. The problem is to explain how ordinary day-to-day language, which exists and lives in and for the world of individuals and objects, may be used meaningfully to refer to this trans-human reality. What does it mean to say that all of existence has a Divine Ground or that God's love is like a father's love? The word "ground" ordinarily refers to the earth beneath one's feet, the word "father" ordinarily refers to one's progenitor, and the word "love" ordinarily refers to a human emotion. When someone asserts that God is Three in One, are they intending to assert such a paradox? Are the above statements at all meaningful, and if so, how and why?

That religious language has a problem has been variously acknowledged by many Western proponents. Anthony Flew merely continued an ancient insight when he suggested that religious statements are not genuine assertions at all. Immanuel Kant noted that many concepts work perfectly well when dealing with a matter of sense-experience but which break down when applied to transcendent realities.

Briefly, we may say that there are two main problems to be resolved regarding religious discourse. First, does language function differently when it is used to make statements about God? Second, how is one to distinguish false statements about God from true ones? Everyone acknowledges that the same language is being used. It is the only language we have. Some, however, believe that ordinary language is not being used in the *same* or ordinary way when one speaks religiously.

This book is an attempt to solve such problems inherent in religious discourse. These problems have existed within philosophy for thousands of years and even to this day there is no one definitive solution. A plethora of literature has grown around this problem giving rise to claims and counterclaims. It is my contention that Advaita Vedānta gives an intriguing insight into understanding religious discourse, or "God-talk" as it has sometimes been called in the Western world. The interpretation that I am proposing, at the very least, does not involve internal contradictions and inconsistencies. Any position is open to attack from "outside." My argument concerns whether a given position is "internally" consistent or not.

Nor do I feel it necessary to describe every possible historical solution. This is important. My intention in stating other proposed solutions is only to give an understanding of, an insight into the problems which all "other" solutions involve. The crux of the issue is, as long as duality is given real ontological value, the problem of religious discourse can never be logically solved. One may take this as my accepted axiom for which absolutely no exception may be made. It is a fact of logical thought and as long as consistent and coherent thought is one's guide, it must be acknowledged and adhered to.

It appears obvious to me that: either there exists a "gap" between the individual and the Divine or there does not. Unless the individual is fully and totally Divine, some sort of gap must exist and with it comes the necessity of crossing that gap. If such a gap exists, then the Divine is an "Other," of one sort or another. This raises the philosophical and existential question of "how does one know an 'other,'" and "is this knowledge veridical or not?"

According to Advaita, the Self, who one truly is, is the proof of everything, including oneself. No "other" can ever be the proof of one's existence because that "other's" existence must be confirmed by you first. One's own being, and knowing, is owed to none outside oneself. It is by imagining others as others that a gap is created. Such a gap need not be bridged or crossed if it does not exist (except in one's imagination). Just don't create it. We have all experienced that the mind can create illusions and the mind can destroy illusions.

Individuals search for proofs for the Truth, proofs for the Self. Advaita claims that asking for such proofs is like a child that demands: "Prove to me that sugar is sweet and only then will I have some." How can a proof of the Truth precede Truth? And will there then be a demand for a proof of the proof?

Advaita avers that philosophical proofs are the work of discursive reason. Yet, for the Advaitin, the Absolute eludes the grasp of discursive reason, of mental concepts. How could the existence and nature of the Self, of *Brahman,* of the Truth be "proved" without turning them into objects? However, an objectified *Brahman*/Self/Truth is a (seeming) appearance of the Absolute and not the Absolute itself.

Where is the dwelling place of Truth/*Brahman*/the Self? Where could one possibly go in search of such a one? And how will one know when one has found it? What is the touchstone which one brings to test it? Religious language, according to Advaita, points to the truth that Truth is not the result of an effort. It is here and now. It is not seen because one seeks for it far away from oneself.

Advaita begins with an enquiry into what is real and what is not real—*nityānityavastuviveka.* Which individual ever questions their cherished belief that they are their physical body, which is obviously born and dies? While alive, externals attract attention and fascinate so completely that rarely does one enquire within. Some Advaitins have compared this to seeing the surface of the ocean and completely forgetting the immensity beneath. Or, like watching the pictures upon a movie screen and ignoring the screen which is permanent and without which the pictures would not appear.

One may identify with the pictures on a movie screen, but it is enough to shift one's attention from the screen to oneself and the spell is broken. While watching a movie, one may identify with the characters on the screen and suffer and rejoice with them. But a simple shifting of one's focus from the screen back to oneself is enough to break the spell. Likewise, one may shift one's attention from the body to an enquiry into one's own Self. Advaita avers that it is due to ignorance that one looks for bliss, for peace, for the Self, in the world of opposites and contradictions. Look within, the "kingdom of heaven" is within.

To posit that the kingdom of heaven is within or that the Self is within is not unique to Advaita. What distinguishes Advaita's vision from other positions is when Advaita asserts that the Self (*ātman*) is not different from the Absolute (*Brahman*). This is the peculiar claim of Advaita and the means whereby it is able to bridge the seeming gap between subject and object, between *That* inscrutable, immutable, seemingly distant Absolute and *this* fallible, mortal, intimately present individual, between God and the human being, between all dualities.

CHAPTER 2

Advaita and Religious Discourse

> Before you ask about ignorance, ask who is ignorant.
> You want to treat the disease before seeing the patient.

CERTAINTY

Traditionally, religious discourse has been involved in a "search for certainty"—for that which will never disappoint, disappear, decay or decline. In recent times, philosophers have turned their attention to the use of religious discourse, but the foundations of faith demand more than this. As will become clear, certain general conditions must be satisfied in order to render religious discourse meaningful. The general idea is that unless some aspect or aspects of religious discourse are indubitable, the entire body of religious discourse can be and will be held suspect.

One instance of this search for certainty was the philosophy of Descartes.[1] Advaita, too, was concerned with a search for certainty and turned Descartes' *"cogito"* upside down. Or, to be more accurate, Descartes turned Advaita's doctrine upside down. Since Advaita was historically prior to Descartes, surely this is one of history's ironic twists of coincidence. Instead of "I think therefore I am," the position of Advaita is, "I am therefore I think." Descartes made the existence of oneself as a thinking being the necessary and indubitable truth from which the rest of his argument proceeded. This presupposition of the *cogito*, however, does not mean that the proposition "I exist" is in any way a necessary truth. In fact, it makes existence contingent upon "thinking."

It is a truth that an individual cannot, without absurdity, doubt one's own existence. And it is necessary to exist in order to form any and every thought, since existence is a precondition for thought. Yet, Descartes' enterprise was an attempt to show that it is a necessary truth that an individual exists as a thinking being.

Descartes wanted to show the indubitability of the proposition "I think." Then, given the fact that the proposition "I exist" is necessarily true whenever one conceives of it, the whole complex of propositions involved in "I think therefore I am" will be indubitable. However, his enterprise failed to accomplish what it set out to do.

Advaita, on the other hand, places its emphasis on the "I" (*Ātman*). Granting the Advaitic definition of the "I" (as the *Ātman*),[2] certainty is gained. Why? Logically this "I" cannot be denied or doubted. It is affirmed by the very act of denial. It is the basis of all proving or doubting. It does not presuppose its own possibility but is the very basis of everything else. In itself it simply is and anyone who questions it, must assume it in order to do the questioning.

The "I" is the foundation of all experience. Anything that is thought or attempted to be described is merely one experience out of an infinite possiblity. Each experience *may* be faulty or misleading. However, whatever may be the experience, true or false, the fact of an experience taking place cannot be denied. It is its own proof. If one is observant, one may observe that whatever be the content of one's experience, the witnessing "I" does not depend upon the content. The "I" is itself and does not change with the event or experience.

Acceptance of the Advaitic vision of the "I" goes a long way because, as a truth, which is beyond the possibility of doubt, it is also a link between itself and ordinary knowledge. Rationalism and Empiricism doubted the possibility of such a link. This "I" (*Ātman*) however, is not based upon human reasoning. Nor is it necessarily dependent upon scriptural authority. It is the pure experience, the pure actuality. It is always immediately given though one does not normally enquire into the content of that "I." All experience is in the mind. But there is no such thing as experiencing the real, the unchanging, the immutable Absolute. The real is beyond experience.

A favorite, convenient, and telling modern example for Advaitins is to note that "when one goes to the movies, one may observe the 'blank' screen or one may observe the pictures playing upon the screen." If one's attention is on the pictures, one does not see the screen, and conversely, if one's sight is on the screen, one does not see the pictures. Interestingly, "picture-fire" does not burn the screen nor does "picture-water" wet it. The unseen base and support of all (the pictures) is forever present even if one never turns one's attention in its direction.

Before anything can come into existence, there must be someone to whom it comes. All appearance and disappearance presupposes a change against some changeless background. The "I AM" can never be changed into the "I AM NOT." Wherever one goes (or doesn't go), one will always find oneself there. This is an obvious truth. It is not so with anything else in one's experience. One is the projector; "others" are the projected.

The word *Ātman* refers to the very substantive being of any conscious being whatsoever which is immediately evident. It is not known through any other sign or symbol. Rather, it is the very awareness to which everything else is an object. It is a literal reference to Reality which is but a matter of direct experience.

What is the Reality which one is attempting to speak about? Is it somewhere else? Is it not (somehow/someway) the very light by which one asks the question and goes in search of the answer? The seeking itself must be That. Non-duality implies that the seeker, the sought, and the act thereof are not different. "I am seeking." "I am the sought." "I am the act of seeking." What is constant throughout and what comes and goes and is adventitious?

One can never meaningfully say, "I am this." It is not possible to know what the Self is, but one can know what it is not. Whatever is pointed out as "this" is not all of oneself. Can there ever be a perception, imagination, and so forth, without you? Experiences belong to you. Experiences come and go. Thus, the Self need not be obtained. One is already the Self. What is "other," alone can be obtained.

Though the "I," as the constitutive Being of the individual, is continually and eternally manifesting itself and is known as the content of the "I"-notion, for it to be consciously known a philosophical-religious enquiry is necessary. The fruit of this enquiry is immediate realization and does not wait for an eschatological verification.

One cannot seriously doubt the existence of one's own self. This is obvious. What is not obvious is the nature of the Self. We will take up this theme a little later, but for the moment let us note the following. The Materialists gave one account of the Self, the Sāṅkhya school another, while the Buddhists yet another.[3] Advaita declared that the empirical self (*jīva*), the self, which is made of the psycho-physical sheaths and which can be objectified, belongs to the realm of appearance. There is, however, the true Self (*ātman*), which transcends the physical realm as well as the realm of all dualities such as subject and object. This Self is not different from the Absolute (*Brahman*).

ADVAITA VIS-À-VIS RELIGIOUS DISCOURSE

We have touched upon a few of the philosophical systems, East and West,[4] which claim to elucidate and endow human life with meaning. However, sooner or later, they all seem to suffer from certain inherent limitations. Their fine-sounding words eventually ring hollow. Not only to others but also to themselves. Not only do their propositions conflict with other proponents but also their claims contain inner contradictions. Modern individuals have found themselves homeless. Words alienate them from themselves, from the world, and from others. They have found themselves estranged in a big world with all of its horizons contracting. Everywhere one turns one is confronted with "the other." The last horizon is the horizon "within."

> Now that my ladder's gone,
> I must lie down where all ladders start,
> In the foul rag-and-bone shop of the heart.[5]

The Advaita Vedāntin's slogan is: "To one's Self; to Self-experience." The Real is involved in, and is the basis of, one's everyday experience.[6] Immanently here and now, the quest begins and ends. Individuals, lost as they are, despair of ever discovering unending bliss and eternal peace. How to reach the horizon of identity now that my ladder's gone? The immense mystery beckons. The age of adventure goes ever on. Where is the final frontier and how to get there?

Conversely, Advaitins claim that to search for Reality is a sham. Where could Reality be but right here, right now? To search means that one is really looking for comfort, which one wants to last forever. But no state of mind can last forever. Nothing in space and time lasts. In the realm of non-duality, everything is complete, right now. Where there is One, no support or proof is needed. Reality need not be pointed at. It can't be said to be "here" or "there." It is not the result of a long effort. It is here and now. It is nearer than the nearest. It is not seen because one looks far away from oneself (outside, in names and forms, in objects and in that which is not one's Self).

THE LOGIC OF RELIGIOUS KNOWLEDGE

The questions which have been raised in regards to religious knowledge in the West have been periodically undergoing revision for the past two thousand years. Now that the reign of analytical philosophy and logical positivism have run their course, no one maintains that language about God is meaningless or merely an expression of an emotion. Now the situation is that a very good case can be made not only for the coherence of religious knowledge but also that all language is multidimensional.[7]

John Macquarrie recently wrote:

> In theological propositions, therefore, we can distinguish more than one dimension or level of meaning and function. Depending on the method (and perhaps also the temperament) of the theologian, one dimension may come to expression more obviously than another, but other dimensions will still be there, though muted and held in the background.[8]

It is my contention that, according to the insight of Advaita, this "reconciliation" still misses the purport of religious statements. To use Macquarrie as an example, he seeks a reconciliation between various statements: Luther's description of God as "that to which your heart clings and entrusts itself is your God" with St. Thomas Aquinas' declaration that God is "He who is," and with Wieman's expression that "God is the behaviour of the universe."[9] Macquarrie's claim is that what we have here is not so much three incompatible points of view as three differences of emphasis.

> When we search below the surface of each formulation, we find that there are implied other dimensions, and that when these are brought to light, they can all be seen as having a place in the unimaginably rich and complex texture of the Being of God.[10]

This Western modern-day "search below the surface" is akin to the Indian idea of "quintuplication" (*pañcīkaraṇa*). Quintuplication is the theory that every physical object contains all the five elements (earth, water, fire, air, ether) in various proportions. A type of theory of "I'll scratch your back if you will scratch mine," or "You can be in my dream if I can be in yours." On the other hand, what Advaita is proposing is that religious knowledge points to that which radically transcends all dualities. And for such knowledge, one must be qualified.

QUALIFICATIONS FOR RELIGIOUS KNOWLEDGE

According to the Advaitin, the path to a proper understanding of religious statements lies in and through knowledge (*jñāna*). The question is: "what is knowledge?" Advaita declares it is not information. It is not about things, people, places, ideas, externals outside. Knowledge is wisdom, which is the Self, within. Knowledge is not a prize for passing some tests. Knowledge is not a reward for good behavior. One is eligible for knowledge because one is knowledge. One need not merit knowledge, it is one's own.

Because one sees "the other" as physical, as a body, one is quick to accuse, condemn, sentence, and execute. The question is: "why begin with others?" Begin with yourself. Advaita declares that the world is non-real and that one's Self is real. Isn't it strange? One says one thing and another hears another. Though the words are the same, there appears to be a gap between speaker and listener, between scriptural injunctions and religious aspirants.

How to close the gap? Give up the idea of being what you think yourself to be and there will be no gap. When one imagines one as separate, a gap is seemingly created. Such a gap need not be bridged—just don't create it. *Ekam evādvitīyam*—one only without a second. How very strange! The very same words which seem true to the sage, to me appear immanently false. "There is no other," how obviously untrue! Thus, the injunction of qualification. To find the Self, it is imperative that one look in the right place; that is, within. Looking outside just won't do it.

Unlike the dictim that "the access to religious discourse does not matter," Advaitin's emphasize the importance and prerequisite of "qualifications for eligibility."[11] Ignorance is acknowledged to be the root of all bondage and can be destroyed only by correct knowledge. By correct knowledge what the Advaitin means is the final, immediate plenary experience of the non-difference of the individual (*jīva*) from the Absolute (*Brahman.*)

The Advaita Vedānta system lays down an oft-quoted, well-known, four-fold requirement,[12] qualifying an aspirant to pursue the path of knowledge. These qualifications are: (1) discrimination of the eternal from the non-eternal; (2) non-attachment to the enjoyment of the fruits of one's actions either in this world or in any other; (3) possession in abundance of the six virtues, *viz.*, calmness, equanimity, turning away from the sense-objects, forbearance, concentration, and faith; and (4) a longing or intense desire for liberation.

According to tradition, only that individual who possesses this four-fold requirement is qualified to study the Vedānta texts under the guidance of a teacher (*guru*), who is not only learned in Scripture but also well-established in Truth. A *guru* is defined as a "spiritual master" who has attained oneness with the Divine and without whom a disciple cannot attain liberation. The path of knowledge (*jñāna*) itself consists of three steps: (1) hearing (*śravaṇa*); (2) reflection (*manana*); and (3) contemplation (*nididhyāsana*).[13] Hearing means the proper understanding of the meaning of Vedāntic statements. These are of two kinds: intermediary texts and major texts. The former relate to the nature of the world, the nature of the individual, and so forth. The latter impart the supreme knowledge of non-duality.

Intermediary texts only impart secondary or mediate knowledge of the truth. It is from the major texts that the direct experience of the plenary reality may be obtained. Though, unless one is a qualified aspirant, even the hearing of the major texts will not produce the plenary experience due to impediments. These impediments are in the form of long-established false beliefs. These false beliefs are to be overcome by reflection and contemplation. When the impediments have been removed, there arises the intuitive experience of non-duality.

HOW RELIGIOUS KNOWLEDGE IS CONVEYED

Not only does Advaita say that an individual must be qualified (*adhikāri*)[14] to pursue the path of knowledge, but also that the Absolute can be known *only* through religious statements (*śabda pramāṇa*).[15] Perception, which reveals the existence of empirical entities, cannot be a source of knowledge of *Brahman*, which is trans-empirical. For one reason or another, all the other valid sources of knowledge (*pramāṇa*) suffer the same fate as perception, with the sole exception of "words as knowledge."[16] There is no conceivable way in which one may come to learn of the non-dual Reality except through religious discourse, that is words as knowledge. This is only common sense and will be made explicit in the chapter on *śabda pramāṇa.*

According to Advaita, the distinctive cause of a valid cognition is a *pramāṇa* (valid means of knowledge). They define a valid cognition as one whose content remains unsublated. Perception and all the other *pramāṇas,* except words as knowledge, produce cognitions which ultimately suffer sublation. (Provisionally, at the empirical level they are accepted as valid but ultimately, at the Absolute level, they do suffer sublation.) *Brahman,* which is the content of the cognition produced by religious discourse, always remains unsublated. Because *Brahman* is eternal, there is no possibility of Its sublation at some later time. Thus, the cognition which religious discourse gives rise to is valid.[17]

There is another point regarding the unquestionable validity of religious discourse. Earlier it was observed that the subject-matter of religious discourse primarily concerns *Brahman.* Perception has been known to betray one in certain cases. For example, a person identifies himself or herself with their physical body and superimposes the attributes of the body upon the Self as when he/she says: "I am lean, male, female, American, Indian, and so forth." Religious discourse informs one that they are neither "lean," nor "male," nor "female," nor "American," nor "Indian," and that the identification of the Self with the body is due to ignorance. It is shown on the basis of knowledge derived from religious discourse that the evidence of perception is wrong. Even simple perceptions revealing that the sun travels across the sky or that railroad tracks come together at a distant point are misleading, as everyone knows. But it can never be shown that what is known through religious discourse is false by relying on the evidence of perception, inference, and so forth, for, according to Advaitic thought, the subject-matter of religious discourse is not open to sense perception.

ADVAITA VIS-À-VIS OTHER SYSTEMS

It should be noted that the essential presupposition and viewpoints of Advaita Vedānta are not those of any other philosophical system. The saying "comparisons are odious," is in a very real sense true. The main thrust of this work is not to compare various philosophical systems' responses to the problems inherent in religious discourse. Its purport is to present a proposed solution which will withstand philosophical scrutiny.

Comparison of an idea in one system by a seemingly similar idea in another system is highly fraught with danger. This is due to the fact that though there is a high degree of general conformity, the two ideas have different associations and contexts which *cannot* be preserved in comparison. Thus, on the one hand, one is led to believe that the comparison has succeeded while, on the other, varying degrees of difference have crept in.

For a general (or superficial) understanding, this discrepancy may not be of great harm. But in philosophy, where accuracy of expression is an essential requisite, the utmost care must be taken to prevent this type of alteration. A loose rendering of a given philosophical term may create serious misconceptions and controversaries.

The point is, any system of philosophy can be correctly understood and appreciated only if it is viewed through the right perspective. If this is not understood, confusion will occur and charges will be leveled, claiming misrepresentation and/or outright distortion.

Some of the presuppositions of the various Indian systems coincide, that is, most Advaitins accept Bhāṭṭa Mīmāṃsa's epistemology,[18] and thus there is a certain use and value in presenting their position. According to tradition, the orthodox systems are coupled and (Advaita) Vedānta is usually coupled with Mīmāṃsā—hence Advaita's other name, Uttara Mīmāṃsā. But unlike Pūrva Mīmāṃsā, with its emphasis on ritual rules, Advaita's task is to teach about *Brahman*.

This study has presented various other viewpoints, not so much from a stance of comparison, as one of perspective. Beyond the apprehension of similarities and dissimilarities, there lies understanding. My aim is the understanding of Advaita's position regarding religious discourse.

THE NATURE OF RELIGOUS DISCOURSE

In this work, I mean by religious discourse: the language of religion, theological language, and depending upon one's perspective, (as will be proposed in this thesis), much if not all of empirical language. Religious discourse is composed of all the utterances of religious individuals regarding their experiences of the Divine. This is a given and usually not questioned. Further, the term "religious" is used as "the universal human ability to conceptualize and concretize the Divine." Divinity is that foundation and basis upon which any and everything exists.

Religious language is generally said to be a reflection upon the languages of religion and seeks to interpret religion and make it both systematic and meaningful. In contrast to this, theological language is said to be indirect and must be inferred, unlike the language of religion which is, in one sense or other, derived from direct experience.

Religious discourse is a varied phenomena. The language of religion must base itself upon either the worldview of language or the viewpoint of ordinary language. Be it noted that both viewpoints are not neutral. Theological language provides one type of setting, and, when the religious tradition changes, the terminology and description also changes, that is, Christian saints speak of their experiences using different language and images than Muslim mystics or Zen Buddhists. Where there are no elephants present, one will not find an "elephant-headed God."

On the other hand, ordinary language is based upon a theoretical description of the world based upon a naive realism. However, we know that the sun neither rises nor sets and to describe time as relative to velocity shocks one's normal perception.

Religious discourse includes not only statements of personal experiences, but also ethical admonitions, creeds, moral codes, ritual procedures, myths, parables, and so on. Religious discourse extends over an almost indefinite range. It appears to arise out of the collective experiences of particular peoples and, does not so much determine what we think, feel, and do as to describe what is thinkable, feelable, and doable.

This work accepts as religious discourse, any and every instance which any individual, anywhere describes as such. The methodological assumption is that religious discourse may be classified into two major divisions for purposes of an initial analysis. Though, in the final analysis, it will be declared that all language, whatsoever, both secular and spiritual, falls into the category of Absolute Language for the Knower of Reality.

In a traditional dichotomy, theologians reflect upon the religious experience while religious individuals express it. Indirect language interfaces with direct language. But in order to make philosophically meaningful statements about this phenomena, so-called direct language must become an Absolute Language. This will become clear later on.

None of these exponents can be understood exclusive to the other. Within the physical realm, the movement is, in the words of the *Upaniṣad,* "from the unreal lead me to the real."[19] Or, to put it another way, the way of outgoing (*pravṛtti*) necessarily precedes the way of ingoing (*nivṛtti*). To sit in judgment and allot marks is ridiculous.

According to Advaita, religious discourse has a two-fold capacity: it can communicate the facts of the empirical world, and it can communicate supersensible truths. Thus, there are two types of religious discourse: secular and scriptural. Further, Śaṅkara said, "The scripture is the only source of knowledge of the truths regarding the suprasensible."[20]

According to the terminology that I employ in this work, from an epistemological or empirical viewpoint, *first-level* religious discourse represents a literal expression directly naming the fact of the non-dual Absolute, for example, "That thou art" (*tat tvam asi*) or "I am *Brahman*" (*aham brah-*

māsmi) and *second-level* language is secondary, indirect, symbolic and/or figurative language. I am also contending that, from an absolute viewpoint or the viewpoint of a supremely qualified aspirant, all discourse is *Absolute* Language, which directly and cognitively asserts the Reality.

First-level religious discourse consists of identity statements or *akhaṇḍārtha vākyas*. Biblical examples of this would include: "I am that I am," or "I and my Father are one." This teaching that *Brahman* and the individual are one is the only direct instruction that can be given to a seeker of the Absolute. There can be no other direct approach to *Brahman* other than knowing It as the Self. Any teaching that does not unveil *Brahman* as the Self of the seeker is indirect, because of its remote reference to *Brahman*. It fails to bring *Brahman* within the reach of the seeker. It is in this sense that the term *"śruti"* reveals its true import. *Śruti* literally means "hearing" that implies a direct teaching. Thus, whatever teaching is direct, that teaching is *śruti*.

Religious language utterances are acknowledged to be of many sorts. Philosophical discussions of religious language have concentrated on a restricted segment of this enormous diversity, namely, theological statements, that is, assertions of the existence, nature, and doings of supernatural personal beings, God, the Absolute. As well, these discussions have centered around the problem of verifiability. Because difficulties have arisen regarding statements which cannot be empirically tested, some philosophers sought nonassertive interpretations. And these latter interpretations have been divided into: expressions of feeling, symbolic presentations, ritualistic interpretations, and myths and mysticism. The main thing to be noted is that, from both a Western and an Eastern perspective, no other system regards, and coherently defends, religious language as a literal expression directly naming the fact of the non-dual reality. Advaita's particular perspective gives rise to at least three startling claims: (1) a non-dual Absolute is more logically consistent than a theistic deity as the referent of religious language; (2) there are first-level statements of religious language directly naming the fact of the non-dual reality; and (3) access to the meaning of religious language statements demands that the seeker possess certain qualifications—without which access to the direct knowledge of *Brahman* is impossible. As well, I make a fourth claim that there is an *Absolute Language* from the unique perspective of a supremely qualified aspirant who has heard and understood the liberating knowledge. Since, to such an individual, "All is *Brahman*," all language becomes religious language.

The identity of the Self (*Ātman*) and *Brahman* cannot be known by any other means of knowledge. The real nature of the Self, beyond the ego, cannot be determined by perception, inference, and so forth. As Śaṅkara said, "Being different from objects of perception, the existence of the Self cannot be proved by this means. Similarly, inference, too, is powerless."[21]

THREE ASSERTIONS

I am putting forth three assertions which, to my knowledge, have never before been claimed in regards to religious discourse. These three claims rest upon the presumption that it is only an Advaitic type of metaphysical and epistemological scheme which can yield a non-contradictory religious discourse. Theistic and/or dualistic visions of God or an Absolute can never be philosophically consistent and noncontradictory.

First, religious discourse is declared to be not only cognitive, but also valid. Advaita claims that the referent of religious discourse is immediately present as the constitutive Being of everything whatsoever, and therefore, self-evident and certain. This means that the referent (*Brahman/Ātman*) is fundamental in a radical sense and prior to all proofs which must necessarily presuppose it. Yet, this referent does not presuppose itself for it is the one indubitable fact of all experience which can never be denied without self-contradiction. There is no other philosophical system can make this type of claim with these consequences.

Second, a two-level theory of language is proposed which claims that there is a first-level language which is a literal expression directly naming the fact of the non-dual Absolute (and that a resort to secondary implication is not necessary). Besides the traditional dichotomy of a two-level theory of language, it is my contention that a case may be made for proposing an Absolute Language which implicitly states that all language directly and cognitively asserts the Reality.

The third contention of this book is that, contrary to a person's generally held understanding, it is more logically consistent to speak of the unqualified Absolute than of a theistic deity. The general idea is that an anthropomorphic God is comprehensible but inappropriate as an object of worship and that a non-anthropomorphic Absolute is utterly incomprehensible. An attempt is made to ground the incomprehensible Absolute within each one's own personal experience thus making it more than a mere assertion or theoretical concept and establishing it as an indubitable fact of personal experience.

It is true that a theistic theologian would claim that the *otherness* of God is experienced directly. However, any relationship with an "other" necessarily implies a given separation, a gap, which no amount of mediation can ever bridge completely. There will always be scope for doubt. On the other hand, an experience that reveals that the subject and the object, the knower and the known, the devotee and the deity are one and non-dual, leaves no scope for uncertainty. Where knowledge is transcended, knowing becomes Being.

CONSEQUENCES

The consequences of religious discourse referring to an "other" means that its approach must be mediated either through perception, reasoning, or religious authority. Philosophically speaking, knowledge thereof becomes, at best, probable and verification highly suspect. Proofs are required for this estranged entity. The individual's goal becomes knowledge *about* and a relationship *with*. This "other" must necessarily be transcendent, concrete, definite, and the Source of all things. It is historically known that these consequences are indefensable from a philosophic scrutiny.

According to Advaita Vedānta, religious discourse refers to the very constitutive Being of anything whatsoever, *Brahman/Ātman*. As such, it is self-evident and absolutely certain. As a "radical empiricism," to know is to be. As the constitutive fact of all experience, it cannot be denied without self-contradiction. When the knower and the known are identical, certainty is inescapable. As such, it is prior to all proofs which must necessarily presuppose it. It is the presupposition, both logically and ontologically, which cannot be denied.

Religious discourse is significant in that it conveys a wisdom enabling an individual to transform oneself from untruth to Truth, from death to immortality. The generally held opinion is that religious discourse refers to some abstract entity floating who knows where? It is my contention that religious discourse refers primarily and ultimately to the individual, here and now.

If the *raison d'être* for religious discourse is linked to the individual's quest for liberation, the religious discourse is primarily a set of rules for self-enquiry and self-mastery. As such, it is useful and true, but in a sense much different from that suggested by Western philosophers. Religious discourse may look like symbols, but it is really empirical. The very use of "I" reveals this.

Self-hood, which is the content of the "I"-notion, is the most immediately known. Though not mediated through the senses, perception of the Self is the most immediate of all. The character of perception is its immediacy and this immediacy is revealed as oneness of Being. Thus, knowing is identified with Being. One knows the Self as the most certain, because one is the Self.

According to Advaita, though the Self (as the constitutive Being of the individual) is always manifesting itself and known as the content of the "I"-notion, for it to be known so consciously, a philosophical enquiry is required. Immediate realization is the fruit of this quest. By bringing the God of pluralistic theism down to the Self-hood of the individual, Advaita renders religious discourse meaningful.

It is not my purpose to give a detailed account of such

metaphorical expressions as, "God is my Father" or any of the other well-known types of religious expressions (though I do concisely analyze a few of these expressions). I am primarily after that which will render a coherent and non-contradictory account of any and every example of religious discourse.

It has been noted that once a relational norm of meaning has fixed the primary function of language to denote something, one's immediate problem becomes one of relating an empirical expression to the seemingly inexpressible. The Mādhyamika solution denied any independent objective referent, and, thus sought to circumvent this problem. However, according to Advaita, Nāgārjuna's position is flawed—though in ways different from the theistic solution's flaws. The crux of the solution lies in the purport of religious discourse.

The purport of religious discourse is the concern of this book. There are various norms for relating words meaningfully. This means that there are more than one or two norms for relating religious discourse as true or false. It also implies something about language's referent or lack thereof.

According to Advaita, the problem of religious discourse is in the final analysis, a pseudo-problem. This is not however, because there is no referent (a la Nāgārjuna), nor because there is no knowledge conveyed by metaphysical propositions (a la Wittgenstein or Strawson), but because the Absolute is One and non-dual. This means that there is no gap between the individual and the Absolute. The knower and the known are non-different.

Since individuals appear to experience the problem of multiplicity, Advaita proposes a self-enquiry and analysis which commences with what one knows, one's own immediate existence, and which culminates with the experience that existence and essence, or the individual and the Absolute, are not different.

Whether one discards everything saying, "not this, not this" (*neti neti*) or one declares that "All names are Thy name, all forms are Thy form" (*sarvam khalvidam brahma*), call it what you will—this is full immersion. Where a gap exists, there quarrels and disputes will exist. But where there is no duality, who is there to quarrel and over what? It is not Reality which must change—merely the way in which the individual looks at it.

CHAPTER 3

Advaita Vedānta—A Perspective

> The seers in the beginning, desiring
> the excellent and searching the
> heavens, embarked upon fervor
> and consecration.
>
> *Atharva Veda* XIX, 41, 1

WHAT IS ADVAITA VEDĀNTA?

Indian philosophy has traditionally been classified in terms of six orthodox (*āstika*) and three heterodox (*nāstika*) schools.[1] In common parlance within India today, a *"nāstika"* means an "atheist." But in this philosophical context, the division into *āstika* and *nāstika* only means an acceptance of, or rejection of, the Vedic corpus as an authority. It is not an exaggeration to say that of these schools, Vedānta in general and Advaita Vedānta in particular have captured the cultural, philosophical, and spiritual imagination of India to an extent unparalleled in Indian thought. Of all the Indian philosophical systems, Advaita has been given preeminence.

By the beginning of the twentieth century, Advaita Vedānta in general and Śaṅkara in particular had begun to receive considerable attention in Europe. This was due primarily to the pioneering work of F. Max Muller and Paul Deussen.[2] Following them, Western studies into Advaita Vedānta's doctrines have received an impetus from the work of such scholars as Paul Hacker, Tillmann Vetter, Hajime

Nakamura, Eliot Deutsch, Sengaku Mayeda, and Wilhelm Halbfass.

Śaṅkara (ca. 788–820 C.E.) is undoubtedly the greatest exponent and consolidator of Advaita.[3] Because it is frequently called the "Advaita of Śaṅkara," this leads to a misunderstanding and one is likely to assume that Śaṅkara was the founder or originator of Advaita. Such an impression is false, though without a doubt Śaṅkara was the greatest expounder of Advaita. In actuality, Advaita speaks of no founder in the sense in which we speak of the founders of other schools, for example, Gautama as the founder of the Nyāya school, Kaṇāda as the founder of the Vaiśeṣika school, Kapila as the founder of the Sāṅkhya school, Jaimini as the founder of the Mīmāṃsā school and so on.

However, this is not to deny that Śaṅkara, as the author of the commentaries (*bhāṣyakāra*), gets the credit for consolidating Advaita and making clear beyond doubt the basic doctrine of Advaita.

> The doctrine advocated by Śaṅkara is, from a purely philosophical point of view, and apart from all theological considerations, the most important and interesting one which has arisen on Indian soil; neither those forms of the Vedānta which diverge from the view represented by Śaṅkara, nor any of the non-Vedāntic systems can be compared with the so-called orthodox Vedānta in boldness, depth and subtlety of speculation.[4]

There is no doubt that Advaita takes its distinctive position vis-à-vis the contribution of its predecessors. Advaita developed its "vocabulary" not only from the Indian scriptures, but also from the Pūrva Mīmāṃsā, Sāṅkhya, Yoga, Buddhist, and Jain philosophies. Advaita developed, at least partially, by polemizing against other systems and in defending its own position. Still, in order to have an insight into Advaita's insights, one is beholden to delve into Advaita's relationship with the *Vedas*. As Natalia Isayeva recently wrote:

> This method revealed some important inner tenets of Advaita, precisely because attention was brought to the role of sacred scripture in Śaṅkara's teaching. It turned out that Vedic texts play a serious theoretical part in securing an inner intellectual balance to his system, valid for every specific problem arising in course of the polemics.[5]

Advaita tradition (*sampradāya*) traces its origins to the *Vedas*. It is not possible to say precisely when Vedic thought began. The *Vedas* themselves contain references to a remote past. With its origins lost in the mists of time, it is "undoubtedly (the) oldest literary monument of the Indo-European languages." There are scholars of the opinion that the *Vedas* were composed around 4500 B.C.E. Others say that the Vedic corpus represents successive stages of development extending over two thousand years with its culmination not later than 1500 B.C.E.[6]

Though scholars differ widely over the exact date of the composition of the *Vedas*—a debate which hardly concerns us here—they could be considered ageless, and this for three reasons.

1. Whatever the date of the *Vedas*, their contents refer to truths which are timeless, eternal, without beginning or end.

> The intrinsic value of the Vedic literature does not, however depend on its hoary antiquity; nevertheless its survival throughout the ages, with little or no interpolation, testifies to its lasting hold on the human mind.[7]

2. As well, the chronological event which solidified the *Vedas* into a body of written sacred texts (by Veda-vyāsa (Kṛṣṇa Dvaipāyana),[8] the arranger or compiler of the Vedic literature as it is now known to us), certainly postdates the beginnings of Vedic thought.

3. And finally, most Mīmāṃsaka and Advaita thinkers consider Vedic truths to be impersonal (*apauruṣeya*) and eternal (*nitya*). Being "authorless" and without beginning or end, Vedic truths recognize neither chronological development nor sublation.

Advaita Vedānta's message could therefore be claimed to be eternal and impersonal. Śaṅkara never seemed to tire of teaching that the *Ātman*, one's inner Self, is wholly non-different from *Brahman*. This was not only the starting point of his thought but also its goal. This Truth he claimed to have found in the *Upaniṣads*. As well, Śaṅkara used philosophy, not as his aim, but the weapon with which to fulfill his aim of rescuing individuals from their "seeming" bondage to liberation.

The foundation of Śaṅkara's message can be directly traced to the *Vedas*, especially that part of the *Vedas* known as the *"Upaniṣads."* The *Upaniṣads* are said to form the concluding portions of the *Vedas*. Thus, they are called *"Vedānta"* (*Veda* + *anta*: end of *Veda*). The term is extremely apt for, like most Sanskrit terms, there is a *śleṣa* or rhetorical figure involved. Sanskrit roots are multi-significant or multivalent. Besides literally expressing the fact that the *Upaniṣads* form the concluding part of their respective *Veda*, the term also expresses the idea that the *Upaniṣads* represent the *aim* or *goal* of the *Vedas*. Being known as the crown or summit of the *Vedas* (*śruti siras*), the Sanskrit word *"anta,"* like the English word "end," may be used to mean both "terminus" and "aim." The aim or goal of Vedānta concerns the nature of *Brahman*.

> In its widest sense, the term *"Vedānta"* means: Vedānta means the *Upaniṣads*, the source of right knowledge, and the *Śārīraka-sūtras*, and other treatises that help to understand their meaning (such as the *Bhagavad-gītā* and the commentaries on the *Upaniṣads*, the *Śārīraka-sūtras*, and the *Gītā*.[9]

The later Vedāntic philosophical schools, including Advaita, derive their name of *Vedānta* from the fact that they claim to interpret the *Upaniṣads*, as well as found their respective systems upon them. The Vedānta (the *Upaniṣads*) are the foundation for the Vedānta (philosophical systems).

The three source books of all the Vedāntic systems, including Advaita, are: The *Upaniṣads*, the *Bhagavadgītā*, and the *Brahmasūtras*. Together these three are known as the *prasthāna-traya,* the triple canon of Vedānta. *Prasthāna* means "foundation" and thus these three constitute the three foundations of: Primary Scripture (*śruti*), Rememberance (*smṛti*), and Reason (*nyāya*). These three are respectively called the *Śruti-prasthāna* (*Upaniṣads*), the *Smṛti-prasthāna* (*Bhagavadgītā*), *and the* Nyāya-prasthāna (*Brahmasūtras*).

The *Vedas* are referred to as *śruti* (that which is "heard"),[10] and since the *Upaniṣads* form part of the *Vedas,* their name as *"Śruti-prasthāna"* is apt. The *Bhagavadgītā stands next to the* Upaniṣads regarding authoritativeness and is considered next in importance. As the *Gītā* forms part of the Indian Epic, the *Mahābhārata,*[11] which is a *smṛti* or remembered text, it is called the *"Smṛti-prasthāna."* The *Brahma sūtras* represent the standpoint of reason because it sets forth the Vedāntic teachings in a logical order.

Thus, we see that the basic source books of Advaita, and therefore its basic doctrine, is based upon *śruti* and supported by *smṛti* and reason. Yet, be it noted that even though Scripture (*Veda*) is the primary and basic authority for Advaita, it does not follow that the Advaitin is a "fundamentalist." Advaita does not follow a blind acceptance or an unthinking belief in scriptural authority. Words convey meanings and the meaning must be correctly understood. Tradition and reasoning play a part in correctly understanding the teaching of Scripture.

There is a famous passage which Advaitins quote again and again: *Śruti, yukti, anubhava.* This saying means that the final court of appeal is experience (*anubhava*)—the plenary experience which is the fruit of enquiry. Scripture is but an indicator of this experience. In light of this, the central teaching of all three source-books is posited to be one and the same by Advaita, that is, *Brahman.* This is cryptically summed up in the statement: *Brahman* is real; the world is non-real; and the individual soul and *Brahman* are non-different.[12]

The central question for Advaita concerns the nature of *Brahman.* The *Brahmasūtras,* which philosophically strings together the central concepts of the *Upaniṣads* in an ordered manner, begins: *"Athāto brahma jijñāsa"*—"Now, therefore, the enquiry into *Brahman.*"[13] And this enquiry is not only intellectual, but also practical. Advaita's thought circles around the theme, *"Ātman* is *Brahman."*[14] Its approach is self-enquiry. Its concern is for individuals, here and now. Its goal is that which is eternally present, immediate, and accessible.

Advaitic tradition claims that it stands for the plenary experience of non-duality. This experience, Advaita further claims, is the culmination of all thought and all systems of philosophy. Advaita can be, and has been, expounded systematically, but, strictly speaking, it is not a system of thought nor a school of philosophy. As Mayeda said, "Philosophy is not his (Śaṅkara's) aim but is rather a vital weapon with which to fulfill this aim, which is to rescue people out of transmigratory existence."[15] Advaita, to an Advaitin, does not mean "monism." It means the truth of "non-duality." The prefix "non" applies not only to duality but also to "isms" and "systems of thought."

The most distinguishing features of Advaita are: The concept of a non-dual (*nirguṇa*) *Brahman* as the ultimate Reality; the doctrine of *māyā/avidyā;* the identity of the individual with *Brahman;* and the conception of liberation establishing the non-difference of the individual with the Absolute.

Advaita posits that there is but one substratum of Reality. This ground is the sole Reality which, in itself, is berift of any attributes or qualities. The appearance of the world is due to the operation of a force called *māyā. Māyā* gives an appearance of reality to the objective world while, in truth, the world has no existence except in ignorance.

This doctrine of Advaita has given many the impression that Advaita claims the empirical world in unreal, illusory, non-existent. This impression stands in need of a great deal of clarification. Advaita never denied that the physical world of plurality appears real enough to those who live within it. Nor would Advaita deny that it makes sense to say that the waking state of consciousness is a public phenomena and can be said to be the "real world" in contrast to the "private life" of the dreaming state. Further, Advaita would agree that within the physical world individuals may distinguish between what appears to be the case and what is actually the case.

Advaita accepts that a datum, any datum, is a datum or perceived object which is irreducible to the perceiving subject. In this sense, epistemologically, Advaita is a realistic school. Still, if there is a level of experience which transcends the subject-object dualism, then, at that level, duality is transcended or sublated. This in no way alters the fact that the subject and object are correlative terms and one should never think of retaining the subject while at the same time reducing the object to the subject. One should never confuse Advaita with various types of subjective idealism. The Self is not a conglomeration of parts, of subjects, and of objects somehow reduced to one giant Self.

Advaita is often spoken of as a type of monism. However, Advaita or non-dualism is not a monism as this term is generally understood in the West. Advaita emphasises "non"; it negates *all* duality and difference. Differences are said to be of three kinds: between members of the same class, between different species, or, lastly, internal differences.[16] A mere monism may not allow the first two types of difference, but it is compatible with the last type. However, Advaita rejects all three types of difference. For this very same reason, Advaitins reject a view of the ultimate Reality as a Person (as is advocated by theism). Thus, to call Advaita "monism," one should be aware that it is really an "absolute monism," or a "complete monism" (so as to distinguish it from all other types of monism).

PERSPECTIVE

To understand, let alone appreciate, any philosophical system, demands that one comprehend its (unique) perspective. It is crucial that one comprehend the distinction that Advaita makes between the Absolute (*pāramārthika*) and the relative (*vyāvahārika*) points of view.[17] This distinction pervades the entire system and what is true from one point of view is not so from another. Without being absolutely clear in regards to this distinction, it is likely that one will accuse the Advaitin of inconsistencies, contradictions, and absurdities.

There are not two types of being nor two truths, but one reality, one truth, as seen from two different perspectives:

> *Brahman* is known in two forms as qualified by limiting conditions owing to the distinction of name and form, and also as the opposite of this, i.e., as what is free from all limiting conditions whatever . . . thus many (*śruti*) texts show *Brahman* in two forms according as it is known from the standpoint of *vidyā* or from that of *avidyā*.[18]

From the empirical point of view, Advaita admits of numerous distinctions. Metaphysically, there is the problem of the One and the many. Individuals are different from one another and there exists a seeming plurality of things. Epistemologically, there is the subject-object dichotomy, as well as the problem of truth and error. Ethically, there is the problem of bondage and freedom. Yet, from the Absolute point of view, there is only *Brahman/Ātman*—One and non-dual.[19]

Either one is involved at the relative level of duality or one realizes the non-dual *Brahman* as the sole reality.[20] The pluralism that is experienced at the empirical level, and with which philosophical enquiry commences, is not the final truth. Advaita admits all kinds of distinctions at the empirical level, from an empirical point of view, yet denies them from an absolute point of view. The uniqueness of Advaita is its doctrine that the relative or empirical level is neither real nor unreal.

Merely because one imagines that they are one small entity in a universe of infinite entities does not make it so. Advaita avers that there is the Self—not "my self," "his self," "her self," and "it self." Because one is misled by the diversity of names and forms, minds and bodies, one imagines multiple selves. Merely because there are bodies present does not necessarily mean that one is a body. The body or mind may be like a room—it is there but one need not live in it all the time. There is space within a jar and outside the jar. To identify with the space within the jar and then to declare that one is limited is a false view of what space is. Merely because one identifies does not make it so.

Advaita avers that anything which is experienced is real, at one level or another.[21] Therefore, Advaita's epistemology is realistic and posits that every cognition points to an objective reference, whether veridical or erroneous. The question becomes: Exactly how real are the things that are experienced in the empirical world? Advaita replies that the things of the empirical world are real so long as the empirical order lasts:

> The division of real and unreal depends upon knowledge or experience: that is real whose knowledge does not miscarry; the unreal on the contrary, is the object of a knowledge which fails or goes astray.[22]

Thus, according to Śaṅkara, the real is that which lasts, which suffers no contradictions, which is eternal and unsublatable. Things of the world may be said to be real until they suffer sublation. Thus, they are called "what is other than the real or the unreal" (*sadasat vilakṣaṇa*), illusory (*mithyā*), indescribable (*anirvacanīya*). Since they are cognized, they are not unreal (*asat*). Since they are sublated, they are not real (*sat*). By this criterion, *Brahman* alone is absolutely real; never being subject to contradiction. All else can be called "real" only by courtesy. The distinction between one individual and another, the existence of a plurality of things, the attribution of attributes to the Absolute are all concessions to the Truth made from the relative point of view.

However, to bring out the full implications of the term *"advaita,"* it should be noted that such expressions as "absolutely real" and "from an absolute point of view" are merely contextual.[23] They are used only by way of contrast with all that is not real. In no other sense can *Brahman/ Ātman* be called real. If one accepts the empirical world of plurality, then such expressions are meaningful. But to one who has realized the Truth, these expressions lose their significance. For such a one, "*Veda* is no longer *Veda*."[24]

The consequence of this "distinction between standpoints" is simple to state and devastating in its implications. At the absolute level, "*Ātman* is *Brahman*."

Where verily there is, as it were, a duality, there one knows another. But when to the Knower of *Brahman* everything has become the Self, what should one know and through what? Through what should one know That owing to which all this is known—through what, O Maitreyi, should one know the Knower?[25]

KEY-CONCEPT

The cornerstone of any philosophical system is that "key-concept' upon which the system revolves. For example, to sustain the radical pluralistic realism of the Vaiśeṣika school, the importance of its key-concept of inherence (*samavāya*) cannot be exaggerated. Likewise, the importance of the internal relation of inseparability (*apṛtak-siddhi*) makes it the key-concept of Viśiṣṭādvaita Vedānta. Within the Dvaita Vedānta school, the concept of difference (*bheda*) is foundational to the system. As well, the concept of particularity (*viśeṣa*) is also basic to Dvaita since Dvaita's radical pluralism finds its justification in specific particulars. Or, to mention but a few examples from Western philosophy, Plato's concept of Form or Idea (*eidos*), Leibniz's *monad*, and Bergson's *élan vital* served as the key-concepts in their respective systems of thought.

The key-concept of Advaita is *avidyā/māyā*.[26] (Since Śaṅkara did not differentiate between *avidyā* and *māyā*, as post-Śaṅkarite Advaitins did, I present the two terms as one key-concept). This entails a little elaboration in order that a familiar misunderstanding does not result. Critics sometimes label Advaita Vedānta as "*māyā-vāda*" and Advaitins are called "*māyā-vādins.*" These terms are used disparagingly and yet there is a grain of truth in the matter. *Avidyā/māyā* cannot exist or function independent of *Brahman* and it ceases to be when *Brahman* is realized. Still, *avidyā/māyā* is the device by which the Advaitin explains how the One Reality appears as multitudenous. Strictly speaking, *Brahman* is the be-all and end-all of Advaita, and if anything, Advaita should be called *"Brahma-vāda."* This is so because Advaita never loses sight of its central doctrine that *Brahman* is real, the world is non-real, and the individual is non-different from *Brahman*. And yet, the concept of *avidyā/māyā* may still be said to be cardinal to Advaita.[27]

What the critics have done is to mistake the means for the end. The reality of *Brahman* is Advaita's sole concern. The Advaitin is not interested in proving the existence of *avidyā/māyā*. Nonetheless, though *avidyā/māyā* is not ultimately real, its importance cannot be exaggerated for the role that it plays within Advaita.

The entire philosophical system of Advaita may be said to be based upon its key-concept of *avidyā*, which is also known as *māyā*.

> *Ātman*, the self-luminous, through the power of his own *Māyā*, imagines in himself, by himself (all the objects that the subject experiences within or without).[28]
>
> . . . .
>
> This unborn (changeless, non-dual *Brahman*) appears to undergo modification only on account of *Māyā* illusion) and not otherwise.[29]

It is by means of this concept that Advaita will delineate its epistemology, metaphysics, and practical teachings. For instance, epistemology presupposes a subject who knows, the object which is known, and the resulting knowledge. The justification and elucidation of this triple form (*tripuṭī*) is accounted for by *avidyā*. Similarly with error, *avidyā* is its material cause.[30] Superimposition (*adhyāsa*) and the theory of illusory appearance (*vivarta-vāda*), which both help to explain the problem of error, presuppose *avidyā*. An inert, material mind needs the help of consciousness for knowledge to arise. Knowledge exists in and through a conscious experience of multiplicity. And it is *avidyā* which is the cause of all these empirical distinctions. The Advaitin contends that the very possibility of empirical distinctions rests upon the existence of *avidyā*.

According to the metaphysics of Advaita, the Absolute is one and non-dual. Thus, arises the apparent problem of the One and the many. What is the relationship between the One and the many, between the Absolute and the relative? The Advaitin must account for the seeming plurality of the universe if the Reality is One and non-dual. An explanation is also called for in regard to the distinction which the Advaitin makes between the Reality with form (*saguṇa*) and the formless Reality (*nirguṇa*). The seeming difference between the individual self and the Absolute needs to be explained. The place of God (*Īśvara*), as well as the creation of the world, must be accounted for. Every Indian metaphysical system endeavours to explain these three entities, that is, the Reality, the individual self, and the physical universe. Advaita must explain how these three entities are really only one. And this Advaita does by elucidating how the concept of *avidyā* is presupposed in each of these issues.

Lastly, the entire practical teachings of Advaita presuppose the concept of *avidyā*. The bondage of the individual, as well as its liberation, hinge upon *avidyā*. *Avidyā* is the root cause of bondage and knowledge is the direct means of its removal. Ethics, aesthetics, and values all have meaning only within the context of *avidyā*. Likewise, all disciplines prescribed for attaining release only become meaningful within the context of *avidyā*.

Next, it must be understood that the metaphysics of Advaita is immanent and not transcendental. This is a key point because it has several far-reaching consequences. Advaita is primarily and foremost an enquiry into the Absolute—an Absolute which is involved in, and is the basis of, the individual's experience. However, though the Absolute is seemingly enmeshed in one's experience, it is not consciously present to one's consciousness like sticks and stones are. The individual must make an earnest enquiry and divine the Absolute through discrimination. Though the Absolute is not something to be gained afresh, it does need to be discriminated from the not-Self. This search is not divorced from experience nor is it outside of one's experience. It comes through an analysis of one's day-to-day experiences, at all levels. This means that at any given stage, an aspirant's qualifications and readiness determine how meaningful religious discourse statements will be.

The vision of Advaita is unique in that its conception of Reality differs qualitatively from all other system's vision. Whether it be Plotinus, Leibniz, Spinoza, Bradley, or Hegel, their hierarchies rest on a quantitative ordering of certain shared or common qualities. Advaita, on the other hand, absolutely denies all dualities. It is not enough to intuit mystically the oneness of all existence. Advaita is neither an intuitive assertion of identity nor a rational synthesis of plurality. It is rather a critical awareness of the falsity of difference.

Advaita's non-dualistic Absolutism is uncompromising. Simply because some Western thinkers have advocated monism, for example, Parmenides, Plato, Spinoza, Hegel, Bradley, Bosanquet, or the unifying vision of mystics, does not mean that there is an exact parallel to Advaita's *Brahman/Ātman.*

Brahman is such absolute Being that it is devoid of any differentiation in the form of a generic or specific difference, or even of any internal difference. It is in this respect that Advaita has no parallel. Even those who advocate a mystical unity go only as far as a doctrine of identity-in-difference. It is felt that an identity without difference would be a pure blank and a mere nothing. Yet, Advaita's vision contends that the Absolute ceases to be the Absolute to the extent it depends on duality and difference. Not only that, but it would follow (under Advaita's contention that "to know" is "to be") that it would be impossible to know or realize the Absolute if there is anything different from it.

Advaita regards the Absolute as that which is foundational to all experience though it is in no sense a substance. It is considered to be that which is different from the phenomenal, the spatial, the temporal, and the sensible. Since all things imply and depend upon it, it is not to be located in space, though seemingly it is everywhere. It is seemingly nowhere since it is not a thing which has spatial relations to anything. Its nature is inexpressible since to say anything about it is to make it into a particular thing.

Advaita's tradition declines to characterize the Absolute in any terms other than in the sense of "secondless," "non-dual." It is in this sense that the terms "Absolute" and "non-dual Reality" are used in this work. There is no English equivalent of the terms *"Ātman"* or *"Brahman."* To translate them as Spirit or Self or Absolute can be extremely misleading for these terms in the English language, for they are loaded with different meanings and connotations from various Western religious and philosophical contexts which (virtually) in no way resemble or equal Advaita's intention.

CHAPTER 4

Advaita Vedānta Prospectus

An ocean, verily, is the word.
Pañcaviṁsa Brāhmaṇa VIII.7.9

RELIGIOUS DISCOURSE—THE PROBLEM

Religious discourse has been called language of a special sort. It is logically odd.[1] It is distinctive and peculiar. It is vague and poetical. It seems to place one between the horns of a dilemma. It has been labeled "meaningless jargon" either because it is useless or else because it is said to be comprised of statements which are *ex hypothesi,* unthinkable and unknowable. The problem may be stated thus: How are we to talk intelligibly about a Divine subject-matter using ordinary, mundane, human language? Religious discourse uses ordinary words of day-to-day discourse in an extraordinary way. For example, when Adam and Eve " . . . heard the sound of the Lord God walking in the garden in the cool of the day,"[2] it is obviously not meant that God has a physical body with which He moves along the footpaths. And to say that "God is good" does not mean that there are moral values independent of, and in relation to which, the Divine can be judged to be good. Is it possible for God to be bad though He succeeds in being good? Is God subject to temptations which He is successful in overcoming? Obviously not. And the Scriptural statement, "It thought, may I be many, may I grow forth,"[3] does not mean that It (*Brahman*)[4] thinks, with a mind, in the familiar secular sense of the word. And the Lord's Prayer is not as clear and simple as it once may have seemed to be. "Our Father, who art in heaven . . . "[5] refers neither to one's parent nor to a place somewhere among the stars. The problem has been stated thus:

> Suppose I am told of a new theological discovery, namely that Brahma wears a hat. And then I am told that it is a divine hat and worn infinitely, since Brahma has neither head nor shape. In what sense then is a hat being worn? Why use these words? I am told that God exists but in a "different sense" of exists. Then if he doesn't exist (in the plain sense) why use that word? Or that God loves us—but in a wholly special sense of love. Or God is a circle whose centre is everywhere and circumference nowhere. But this is then to have neither a centre nor a circumference and hence not to be a circle. One half of the description cancels out the other half. And what is left over but just noise?[6]

There must exist a justification for this special use of ordinary mundane terms. If words which are applied to the objects of religious discourse do not have the same meaning as when applied to the objects of ordinary mundane language, then the exact nature of those objects becomes difficult to define. Statements containing such words will be unthinkable, for no intelligible content can be assigned to them. The more this aspect of the dilemma is asserted, the closer one finds oneself to agnosticism. Or, on the other hand, if one asserts existence and causality to the objects of religious discourse in a similar sense (not necessarily identical) in which they are asserted to the objects of ordinary language, used in a common mundane way, then such language becomes redundant and useless. The more similarity is emphasized, the nearer one approaches towards anthropomorphism. Thus, the Divine Reality begins to recede, and with it recedes the very essence for which religious discourse was deemed necessary in the first place.

> Whether we set out from human language with the intention of talking about God, or whether we set out from the

reality of God in order to discover how he can be expressed in human language, we might come to an impassable gulf.[7]

Thus, we are presented with a serious problem. How does religious discourse derive its use/meaning from ordinary mundane language? Until this problem is solved, the exact meaning which religious discourse is asserting will remain vague and unclear. If religious discourse consists of assertions of facts, then such assertions may turn out to be meaningless. This could be attributed to the unverifiable nature in terms of sense-experience of the objects of religious discourse. Alternatively, to say that religious discourse is a set of metaphors may shed no light on the problem either. The question will remain as to what do the metaphors refer to. " . . . metaphors must have translatability into non-metaphorical meanings. Else, they become meaning-less and arbitrary because non-experiential terms can never be understood."[8]

Another way of saying this is to note that talk about God, the Absolute, however one wishes to word it, is not ordinary talk. It is incomparable for a number of reasons. It has no point of reference, no basis above or outside itself. This renders it mysterious. It is neither a thing nor a non-thing. It is the limit, the barrier, the ground or source from whence all else proceeds and takes meaning.

INDIRECT APPROACHES

According to Advaita epistemology the secondary or indirect meaning of a word (*lakṣyārtha*) is necessarily connected with its primary meaning (*mukhyārtha*), and operates only when the literal sense is unintelligible.[9] All words have their own explicit primary meaning which is directly conveyed by the words themselves. The secondary meaning is resorted to only when the primary meaning does not do full justice to the context. However, it must be noted that even when the secondary meaning is understood, the primary sense of the word is never forgotten. Thus, the special extension of the primary, ordinary sense of the word must always have its justification only in the context of the relevant situation, and with direct reference to the primary meaning. In regards to religious discourse, usually those words which function in both an ordinary mundane context and, also a religious context, primarily signify a secular meaning. Ordinarily it is this secular meaning which developed first and which determines the common definition of the word. When such a word is then employed in religious discourse, its meaning is an adaption of the primary secular meaning.[10] And here lies a problem. The objects of religious discourse are not experienced through the senses and thus how can it be established that the metaphorical meaning is necessarily connected to the non-metaphorical meaning?

If the objects of religious discourse are not experienced through the sense organs, then such language must be composed of a set of symbols. However, the dilemma of symbolic language is that there should be a non-symbolic access to the symbolized. With regards to religious discourse this passage seems to break down. Does one know what the symbol stands for before employing the symbol? If so, there is no necessity for employing symbols. Yet in regards to religious discourse, its very subject matter seems to preclude such a knowledge.

The doctrine of analogical predication fails because it is unable to bridge the gap between what it conceives of as radically different entities, that is, God and individuals and the world. The Indian theory of secondary implication will be seen to resemble the doctrine of analogy in that something is being said, but not literally. A major drawback to this is that much of the force of the original statement goes out of it if whatever is being claimed cannot be stated literally as well. Or such is the claim of the Empiricists/Positivists.

If God is non-anthropomorphic, great philosophical difficulties arise as to what can be meaningfully said about a non-symbolic Ontological Being. Certainly a statement like "God created the world" seems intelligible. And inferences can be drawn from it, that is, if God created the world, it is not uncreated, it just didn't happen, and so forth. This shows that there is some understanding going on and yet there still doesn't necessarily show that the original statement has any intelligible meaning itself.

THE GAP

How to bridge the apparent gap between ordinary language and religious discourse? Seemingly, whether one begins from either the common, mundane empirical side or whether one begins from the exhaulted, incomparable Divine side, the gap remains unbridgeable (except perhaps by an arbitrary leap). Does there exist a bridge which can withstand the challenge posed by the problem of religious discourse? Regular users of religious discourse do not seem to be perplexed by this so-called gap. They sing, and pray, and read the Scriptures, and listen to religious discourses without getting lost in the by-lanes of philosophical analysis. Though, they, too, may become puzzled when they are pressed to explain "just what exactly do you mean by that?" or "is your statement to be taken as literally true?" Many attempts have been put forth to explain or explain away this difficulty. These attempts range from labeling religious discourse as figurative, or mythological, or eschatological, or pragmatic, or paradoxical, or contextual, or performative, or factual, or absurd, or odd, or informative, all the way to calling it the Word of God.

Tradition in almost all religions declares that God or the Absolute is ineffable. The classic doctrines wax eloquent about that which is supposed to be unspeakable. Likewise many modern linguistic philosophers are concerned with what can and cannot be expressed in language. Following the lead of Wittgenstein, to speak of the unspeakable is a contradiction in terms.[11] It seems that there is a prima facie case against religious discourse in attempting to say something about that which in principle nothing can be said. And not only can one ask whether one can speak about the unspeakable, but also whether there is really something which is beyond language at all. In fact, the main thrust of the sceptic's attack is not in asking whether one should speak of the unspeakable, but in asking whether there is really something whereof one cannot speak. If there is an ineffable Absolute, how does one know such? And conversely the question may be posed, if one denies that there is an ineffable Reality, how does one know what one is denying and why is it necessary to deny it at all?

Frederick Streng put forward the thesis that the Ineffable may be approached from three different structures of religious apprehension: a mythical structure, an intuitive structure, and Nāgārjuna's dialectical structure.[12] The first two approaches presuppose that there is some sort of Absolute to which they refer, while Nāgārjuna, on the other hand, denies the existence of any independent referent whatsoever.

While Advaita agrees that there is no *external, objective* referent in actuality, one must be very careful in understanding what *Brahman* actually is. It is my contention that Streng's mythical and intuitive structures of religious understanding come under a category of second-level language or, indirect understanding. As shall become clear later on, if one differentiates the intuitive structure into two types, one type will reflect a first-level language and the other one will reflect a second-level language. Yet, neither paradigm reflects, under my classification, Absolute Language.

Both mythic and intuitive language try to say something about the ineffable Reality. Advaita agrees with Nāgārjuna that this Reality is not an essence with attributes. However, Advaita criticises any understanding of *Brahman,* which contends that it is a bare nothing, a contentless blank. Nothing conceptual can be said *about* the Reality because it transcends all empirical categories. Still, there is no contradiction is speaking about the Ineffable-as-unspeakable or beyond categorization because what the term (Ineffable) suggests is not that one is forbidden from speaking, but that what one is speaking about is transcendent to all thought.

Advaita denies a totality of all individual phenomena, as well as particular forms, as being the "object of apprehension" or referent. This is an idea similar to what Nāgārjuna professes. But unlike Nāgārjuna, who takes his stand upon a particular interpretation of *emptiness,* Advaita takes its stand upon *Brahman*. (whether *"emptiness"* and *"Brahman"* are the same or not is another matter altogether and one which will not concern us here.)

RELIGIOUS DISCOURSE—ITS "USE"

It is a curious matter that philosophers from ancient times up to the present day speak of the ineffability of religious discourse in some form or other. Though it is true that the Upaniṣadic sages spoke differently than the Judeo-Christian adherents, who again spoke differently than Wittgenstein or Nāgārjuna, the contention runs throughout religious discourse that although silence is the most eloquent statement about the Ineffable, philosophic discourse does have a use.

This point is important to note for a variety of reasons. Advaita is often challenged on a number of fronts. How can an ontologically unreal Scripture produce a real effect, that is, liberation? How can a never-to-be-encountered attributeless Reality be spoken of at all? If all is unreal, why talk of effects and uses?

If one does not speak, one is open to the charge of ignorance. And, on the other hand, if one speaks about that which is declared to be unspeakable or ineffable, one is open to the label and charge of inconsistency and contradiction. If the subject matter of religious discourse is indeed ineffable, then perhaps St. Augustine was correct in saying, we speak of God "not in order to say something, but in order not to remain silent."[13] Likewise Śaṅkara refers to an Upaniṣadic passage wherein a seeker, Vāṣkalin, questions the teacher, Bāhva, about *Brahman*. Three times the question is put forward and three times Bāhva remains silent. Finally Bāhva says, "I am teaching you, indeed, but you do not understand. Silent is the self."[14] This implies that there is a Reality, that this Reality is teachable, and that the nature of this Reality is inexpressable. And finally there is the *locus classicus* of this problem which occurs in the *Bṛhadāraṇyaka Upaniṣad*. Gārgī puts Yājñavalkya between the horns of a dilemma. If he explains *what Brahman* is, he will be guilty of contradicting what he has already stated about the ineffability of *Brahman*. And yet if he doesn't answer her question, he will be open to the charge of non-comprehension. To escape this dilemma, Yājñavalkya gives the famous *"neti-neti"* (not this-not this) reply and declares that this is what the knowers of *Brahman* have said.[15] In the modern-day world, ravenous for mass communication, the fact that tradition says that God loves obscurity does not engender religious discourse any easier to digest.

PECULIARITIES OF RELIGIOUS DISCOURSE

As long as religious discourse has been used, it has been acknowledged that it possesses peculiarities and an obscurity not attendant to ordinary, common everyday language. That it is sometimes "odd" or paradoxical no one would deny. And no philosopher today will dismiss religious discourse as meaningless thereby. However, it is incumbant upon the users of religious discourse to show in what way it does possess a meaning in spite of, and along with, its admitted obscurities.

What does one mean when one employs the concepts found in religious discourse? Is there an intelligible sense in such a usage? Even before one can discuss the truth or falsity of such statements, their meaning must be known, however vaguely. Logical Positivism gave way to linguistic analysis and it is now commonly accepted that there are many levels of language. Each level has its own reason to be. And yet, like Quine said, one should be concerned with their "irreducible posit" and the part that language plays there.[16]

It was once fashionable for the Positivists to propound the doctrine that whatever one wants to say, can be said—briefly and clearly. Today such a Procrustian bed is seen as nothing more than a methodological presupposition foisting a dogmatic criterion of meaning upon conceptual analysis. By arbitrarily assuming one type of language as paradigmatic—a naturalistic one in which the physical is given primacy—they had fabricated by fiat what they set out to prove. Today, linguistic philosophers no longer automatically rule out religious discourse as meaningless jargon. But they still submit it to an analysis, centering their concentration upon particular concepts used therein, focusing especially upon the elusive concept of "God."

As well, it is generally conceded that religious discourse is of many kinds. It has linguistic uses such as praying, commanding, promising, imploring, and so forth, as well as descriptive or fact-stating uses such as giving historical records, epistemological and metaphysical positions, and so forth. It is also evident that there exist cognitively meaningful statements which are quite literal and informative and which are not even remotely verifiable, that is, "pass the salt," or "what time is it?" But even accepting that there are a multiplicity of languages with a diversity of meanings, the question still remains, what does a particular statement mean? Labeling statements as prescriptive or descriptive does not necessarily reveal their meaning and the basis behind it. What is being claimed and what does this claim entail?

The problem of the meaningfulness of religious discourse is by no means a contemporary phenomenon. It has attracted the attention of philosophers, both in the East as well as in the West throughout the ages. Over two thousand years ago Plato wrote:

> The father of all this universe is past finding out; and even if we found him, to tell of him to all men would be impossible. . . . If, then, Socrates, amid the many opinions about the gods . . . we are not able to give notions consistent with one another, do not be surprised. Enough, if we adduce probabilities as likely as any others.[17]

Similarly, it was said in the *Upaniṣads:*

> The eye does not go there, nor speech, nor mind. We do not know (*Brahman* to be such and such); hence we are not aware of any process of instructing about It. That (*Brahman*) is surely different from the known; and, again, It is above the unknown. That which is not uttered by speech but that by which speech is revealed, know that alone to be *Brahman,* and not what people worship as an object.[18]

However, language and the problems it presents, have resurfaced as an important contemporary philosophical issue in the Western world with the advent of the "linguistic turn."[19] By this is meant, ever since the view was proposed that philosophical problems are solvable (or dissolvable) either by reforming language or by understanding better the language that one uses. In contrast to this relatively recent emphasis given to linguistics and the philosophy of language in the West, Indian philosophy has an unbroken history of linguistic speculation which precedes recorded history and continues unbroken up to the present time.[20] And unlike so many Western proposals which reduce language either to a mere human convention having only scientific or factual referents, or which reduce the meaning of ordinary language to the level of obscure mysticism,[21] Indian philosophy has always postulated both an empirical, as well as a metaphysical dimension to language. A careful analysis has been made concerning the physical properties as well as an investigation into the meaning and inner aspects of language. For example, Bhartṛhari (A.D. 580) opened his *Vākyapadīya* with a metaphysical investigation centered on the relation between *Brahman* and the origin and nature of language.[22] Then he proceeded to investigate the technical aspects of grammar as involved in the everyday use of language. Thus, according to the Indian tradition, language has the ability to relate to the empirical world and yet at the same time, to suggest the highest metaphysical conceptualizations. And some schools therein, like Advaita Vedānta, propose that language conveys the common link between the individual and the Absolute.

THE THEME OF ADVAITA VEDĀNTA

The theme of a particular science ought to be that which is not treated of in any other science. Epistemologically, Advaita Vedānta states this as: "Valid knowledge is that knowledge which has for its object something that is not already known (and is uncontradicted)."[23] The theme of Advaita, and its uniqueness as well, lies in it uncompromising declaration that: "*Brahman* is real, the world is unreal, and the individual self and the supreme Reality are not different."[24] This theme is said to be conveyed through Scripture (*śruti*) by means of the methodological tool of religious discourse. And therein lies a problem. How can a finite individual self and the Supreme Reality be identical? Scripture seemingly makes meaningful statements about an entity which Scripture itself alleges to be trans-sensual. And if this is the case, religious discourse should necessarily fail to convey such, for there is an inherent, inbuilt limitation in words to express the inexpressible. The problem is to explain how ordinary day-to-day language, which exists and lives in and for the world of individuals and objects, may be used meaningfully to refer to this trans-sensual supreme Reality.

ŚAṄKARA'S SOLUTION

A possible solution to this problem was presented through the genius of Śaṅkara. What as propounded was a radical transvaluation of the Hindu Scripture. From what appeared to many as a seemingly mass of meaningless jargon, Śaṅkara transposed the Scripture into a meaningful means of communication of the highest import. His declaration was that the Scripture primarily concerns individuals, here and now, and not a God, above and beyond. It refers to that which is immediately evident and immanently present, that is, the innerdwelling Self. Contesting the fact that all language qua language is inherently inadequate to express the inexpressible, religious language has the unique character of being a report of those who have intuited the inexpressible directly in religious experience. Religious discourse is thus a direct informant of Reality which is radically but a matter of direct experience. Moreover, religious discourse has another unique feature which distinguishes it from other types of language in that it possesses the ability to awaken this experience to a greater degree than other languages do—even as a nightmare possesses the ability to awaken a sleeping individual to a greater degree than any other type of dream. The content and purport of a nightmare encourages a person to awaken from sleep so as to end the frightening dream. In a similar manner, that language which is defined as religious, especially the Great Sayings (*mahāvākya*) has a greater power to awaken a person from the dream of worldly life (*samsāra*) than other types of language.

It is this insight which empirically anchors the Advaitin's conception of religious discourse. Certain scriptural statements have an immediate reference to the very depths of one's being, the Being of all being, and thus point to the most empirical of all. More than any other type of language, religious discourse refers to the radical roots of anyone and everyone and thus it has an immediate relevance to everyone's life as well.[25] The Scripture declares the royal road to self-mastery through knowledge born of self-enquiry. And it is through an analytical study of human experience that this empirical foundation will reveal itself.

To interpret "empiricism" and "experience" in the narrow restricted meaning of sense-experience, as the Positivists do, is arbitrarily to eliminate a very wide range of data that comes to individuals through various types of experiences. There is no valid reason, other than as an arbitrary personal opinion, to dismiss on empirical grounds, religious discourse as meaningless jargon dealing with some supra-empirical entity or entities not subject to empirical verification. Because religious discourse is grounded upon experience, in the most complete sense of the term,[26] its subject-matter is foundational to each and every attempt of verification by experience.

Waking sense-experience is neither self-explanatory nor complete as a source of knowledge. It proceeds under the circumscribing methodological presupposition that only certain realms of phenomena are fit to be explored and all the rest are to be excluded. Gauḍapāda (A.D. c. 6th century), the first systematic exponent of Advaita Vedānta, maintained that dream experiences are on a par (ontologically) with waking ones. Dream objects are as real to the dreamer as waking objects are to one who is awake. Though dream states do not conform to waking states, they do form a similar class of experiences and within that class they are equally coherent.[27] It is irrelevant to object that dream water does not quench one's waking thirst. Dream water quenches a dream thirst and thus the experiences within either the waking or the dream state are equally real and valid within their own orders respectively.

Dreams are real as long as one dreams and waking experiences are real so long as one is awake. To object that dream experiences are subjective and not objective (like waking experiences) is to miss the deeper significance underlying both types of experiences. An analysis of the states of waking, dreaming, and deep sleep will reveal that all three of them are impermanent and thus, to the Advaitin, unreal—though not non-existent.

However, the Advaitin perceives as underlying all of these three states, and persisting throughout, a permanent Self (see *avasthā traya vicāra*). A purely objective approach will land one in materialism and atheism. A purely subjective approach lends itself to the logical conclusion of subjectivism, solipsism, and scepticism. Thus, is demanded a synthetic analysis of the objective, external world along with the subjective, internal world.

Advaita Vedānta approaches all of life with its emphasis on self-enquiry. Scriptural statements may appear to look analogical, symbolical, and/or metaphorical, but according to the Advaitin, their basis is directly, immediately, and empirically rooted. Their concern is with individuals here and now. Their content is with the depth of one's own being. They have a literal reference to the Reality in that they relate to that which is eternally present, immediate, and accessible.

Scriptural statements make suggestions for a self-enquiry. Their role is informative. They are useful and true in that they lead to self-knowledge. And self-knowledge is release (*mokṣa*). Thus, the individual must perform a rigorous inward search. This enquiry will lead to self-knowledge. And self-knowledge is immediate. Thus, instant is the light with which we see.

There is a commonly accepted presupposition in Western

philosophy which draws a distinction and strict dichotomy between language and the Absolute. Whether Socrates or Aristotle, Russell or Wittenstein, Quine or Chomsky—they have all sought to bridge the gap between language and Reality. In apposition to this view is that put forth by the Advaitin which posits that Reality is not fixed behind language—all the while remembering that language is part and parcel of the empirical world. Scripture does not speak of *Brahman* as an object—it only removes one's ignorance of *Brahman*.

ADVAITA AND LANGUAGE

The Upaniṣadic tradition, which is the foundation upon which Advaita takes its stand, declares:

> This *Brahman* indeed shines forth, when one speaks with language.
> *Kauṣītaki Upaniṣad* II.13
>
> . . . .
>
> The ultimate abode of language is *Brahman*.
> *Ṛgveda* I.1.164
>
> . . . .
>
> Language is *Brahman*.
> *Bṛhadāraṇyaka Upaniṣad* IV.1.2

Here is an example of the truly Indian mannerism which seeks to understand anything in both is phenomenal and transcendental aspects. One aspect demands analysis while the other demands contemplation. Seemingly incompatible, the dilemma is resolved by a reference to perspective.

The distinction between religious discourse and ordinary language or non-religious discourse is a derivative one. After all, language is language. To conceive of language as symbolic may be to preserve realism, but this does not account for everything. While, on the contrary, if language is literal, that is, language = *Brahman*, the symbolic has no place.

Thus, there is recognized a place for individuals immersed in ignorance and individuals not different from the Reality. Advaita is built upon the doctrine that knowledge of *Brahman* is real and possible through the vehicle of (religious) language. The distinguishing fact to be always remembered is that this "knowledge" is not knowledge of an "other," that is, God, but Self-knowledge.

CHAPTER 5

Methods and Perspectives

> Writing always means hiding something in such a way that it is then discovered.
>
> —Italo Calvino

INTRODUCTION

We have noted that there are problems inherent in religious assertions. Philosophers in general and linguistic philosophers in particular are concerned with what can and cannot be expressed in language. What do the words used in religious discourse mean and what function(s) do they play? Are they cognitive, factual, and verifiable or are they non-cognitive, non-factual, and unverifiable?

This work presents two paradigmatic approaches to these questions. Either religious discourse refers to an "other" and the approach to this remote and foreign "other" must be through perception or mediated concepts; or religious discourse refers to the very constitutive Being of anything whatsoever and as such is self-evident, immediate, and certain.

The problem of verbal expression of religious themes is both complex and varied. It may be approached from different perspectives. Joachim Wach pursued it along the lines of structure, content, and function.[1] Mircea Eliade pursued it along the lines of archetypal patterns expressing the sacred.[2] Frederick Streng postulated three structures of religious apprehension.[3] T. R. V. Murti identified two principal traditions: the Naturalistic and the Brāhmaṇical.[4]

My approach is meant to be one out of many possible approaches. My aim is to discover if there is an avenue which allows for a consistent and non-self-contradictory interpretation concerning the employment and expression of religious discourse.

The problem of religious discourse is important because it questions not only the meaningfulness of language but also whether empirical expressions can relate to the extra-empirical. As well, it raises the question if there is even an extra-empirical Reality at all.

METHOD

Indian philosophy in general and the Vedāntic systems in particular aim at discovering an ultimate unity which runs throughout the universe of multiplicity. Through its analytical emphasis, Advaita Vedānta is searching for more than a mere theoretical construct. It is in pursuit or search for that which is eternally real and existent and common to all, and to which all of one's epistemological conjectures should correspond. Advaita Vedānta calls this unity the foundation of all. As the Being of all beings, it logically must be one and non-dual, eternal, immediate, and immutable. Such a unity cannot be a partial harmony or an aggregate. It cannot be established by fusing individual particulars together. Entities held together by a coherence or a *genus* that includes all species is but a temporal fusion. And that which can be put together, can be broken apart. That which is born will die. Thus, Advaita's unity is a denial of duality from the very beginning itself.

Further, Advaita posits that this Reality can be known only through that aspect of "word as knowledge" (*śabda pramāṇa*) known as the Scripture (*śruti* or Vedic testimony).[5] Those who want to know the Reality must make an enquiry.[6] "Without enquiry, the sacred teaching is incapable of generating *Brahman*-knowledge."[7] And it must be kept in mind that this does not imply a dogmatic idolatry of the (Indian) Scripture. Scripture is assuredly the only means for the knowledge of the Absolute, but it is not just any Scriptural statement that is meant. As Vācaspati Miśra said, "It is purportful Scripture that is authoritative, and not Scripture as such."[8] And purportful Scripture is any statement, past, present, or future which reveals the identity of the individual self and the supreme self as the non-dual Absolute. *Śruti* is but the name and description given to Scripture which reveals such—thus the Christian declaration, "I am that I am," or "My Father and I are one" would equally fulfill these criteria.

The nature of the role that religious discourse plays in Advaita Vedānta is unique. Reality is of the existent and knowledge of this Reality is said to be object-dependent (*vastu-tantra*). Thus, Reality can be known only if one uses a correct means of knowledge. Or, to state this otherwise, the means of knowledge to be used will depend upon the nature of the reality to be known. Knowledge is declared to be controlled by the already existent reality.[9] Thus, the knowledge which words as knowledge gives, as of all knowledge, is revelatory and merely informative.[10] Its function is merely to reveal the nature of the thing. And the nature of a thing is by definition, eternal. It is what it is. Otherwise, if it changed, it would be other than what it is. Knowledge must answer to that nature. "Knowledge is an agreement of thought with reality."[11] It is controlled by the already existent reality and thus is independent of circumstance, time, place, and so forth. It has to follow the nature of the object as it is. An object is independent of one's knowing it and to misrepresent it is to commit an error. Thus, for words as knowledge (*śabda pramāṇa*) to be a source of valid knowledge, it should fulfill two conditions: It must intimate what is otherwise unknown, and what is made known by it should not be contradicted subsequently.[12]

These two conditions *śabda pramāṇa* fulfills, for the knowledge of *Brahman* which it conveys is not otherwise known and as *Brahman* is eternal and immutable; knowledge of it is never sublated. *Brahman* being an established fact, is established independent of anyone knowing it. Yet the knowledge of *Brahman* will arise only through religious discourse since *Brahman* is not a sensible or even thinkable empirical object. One would never even conceive of seeking *Brahman* were one not introduced to it through the Scripture.

However, the question arises as to exactly how this knowledge of *Brahman* is conveyed. Religious discourse has recourse to ordinary words and their meanings to reveal the Reality. How are common words able to indicate this Reality when it is said to be free from all qualities, actions, class features, and relations? An established fact is said to be known through sources of knowledge like perception. Yet the nature of Reality defies any description in terms of the categories known to thought. There is nothing similar to the Absolute, dissimilar to the Absolute, and there is no internal differentiation within the Absolute.[13] How can an ineffable, unconceivable to thought Reality be revealed by thought?[14]

Advaita replies that *Brahman* is an established fact and that an established fact may be perceptible or not. Perceptibility is not the criterion for an established fact existing prior to the sources of knowledge. Though, that such an entity exists, is learnt only from religious discourse and realized in experience as one's own self. Since *Brahman* is non-dual and exceedingly subtle, there is no other means of discovering it. Still, religious discourse doesn't say that *Brahman* is such and such, "this" or "that," so much as to reveal that it is not an object of any kind. There is no contradiction in speaking about the unspeakable because the Absolute transcends all empirical categories but does not forbid saying such. *Brahman's* ineffability means that it is to be known differently than one knows things empirical. Once the distinctions of the knower, the known, and the resulting knowledge are rooted out, *Brahman* will be revealed as an ever-existent, self-luminous fact.

Advaita Vedāntins employ at least six different methods by which to convey "self-knowledge" linguistically. One such method is described by Śaṅkara in his commentary on the *Bhagavadgītā.* This method has been time-honoured in the Advaita tradition as the traditional method for teaching the trans-phenomenal *Brahman*.[15] It employs the technique of prior super-imposition and subsequent denial (*adhyāropa* and *apavāda*). First, qualities and relations like omniscience, omnipotence, omnipresence, causality, and so forth, are superimposed upon the Absolute so as to enable one to form some sort of understanding. Then, gradually these attributes are negated as a deeper and deeper analysis is performed. From the familiar, one is led to the unfamiliar. From the known, one is led to the unknown. As Śaṅkara put it: "Their aim (religious knowledge) is to be the means of detachment from the objects towards which one is naturally attracted."[16]

A second method, which goes hand in hand with the above technique, is the method of *via negativa*. The *Bṛhadāraṇyaka Upaniṣad* says, "Now therefore the description (of *Brahman*): 'Not this, not this.' Because there is no other and more appropriate description than this 'not this.'"[17] Śaṅkara, commenting on this passage, says that the Absolute can never be properly denoted by any words—including the word "Absolute" (*Ātman*). Thus, the only appropriate way to indicate *Brahman* is to say, "not this, not this." Though no positive description of the Absolute is possible, Śaṅkara claims that a negative characterization may be comprehensible. Its import is not so much to say that there are no characteristics applicable to the Absolute as to indicate the impossibility of attributing any conceptualization to it. Thus, it becomes a linguistic device to avoid categorical mistakes. It is a methodological language-symbol, which draws attention to the ineffability of the Absolute. Thus, "not this, not this" has been called a way or manner of expounding the Truth.[18] Religious discourse is a conceptualization of that (of the Reality) that is destroyed as soon as it is conceptualized in thought. Yet conceptualization is necessary and cannot be avoided if self-knowledge is to arise. Thus, one must use the concept in such a way as to recognize this paradoxical situation.

A third technique consists in the use of metaphor and rhetoric. *Brahman* is said to be known through implication (*lakṣaṇā*). *Words can signify either a class characteristic, a quality, an action, or a relation.*[19] However, none of these factors, which occasion the usage of words, are present in *Brahman*. Therefore, *Brahman* cannot be known by the express meaning of words (*vācyārtha*). Thus, it is concluded that statements made in the Scripture must be interpreted in their secondary implication. Even such positive expressions as "*Brahman* is reality, knowledge, and infinity"[20] are to be interpreted as being positive only in form. The words are understood rather by what they negate than by what they affirm. Their significance is to be understood only as a denial of the contrary meanings of the terms. Thus, the Absolute is that which is not non-being, not what is inert, and not that which is related to sorrow. This method declares that it is the purport of the significance of the terms which is the deciding factor in determining their meanings. (Though this technique is well-known and made much use of by Advaitins, there are those who deny that one need resort to a *lakṣaṇā—both in what I will term first-level language as well as in second-level language.*

A fourth possible method of conveying the knowledge of Brahman is through a direct hearing of purportful Scripture. For someone adequately qualified (*adhikārī*), the hearing of an impartite sentence (*akhaṇḍārtha vākya*) produces direct knowledge. Though on the surface of it, an impartite sentence may look contradictory, there is no need to resort to secondary implication. It is only the philosophers and those not qualified that need to resort to other interpretations in order to render such statements meaningful.

Another possible technique, according to the Advaitins, is by the use of etymology.[21] The word *Brahman* etymologically derives from a root signifying greatness. Greatness implies limitlessness and from this ideas like eternality, purity, and so forth, follow. By amplifying this train of thought, one comes to know more and more about *Brahman*, that is, one approaches closer and closer to *Brahman*-knowledge. Such an enquiry leads to a belief that such a Reality is not only possible but also a possibility. The acceptance of such a conception fosters further enquiry which eventually will lead to the realization of *Brahman* itself.

A final possible technique for conveying *Brahman*-knowledge is silence.

> How strange! Under the banyan tree are old men. Their teacher is only a boy. His explanation consists in silence. Yet the disciples have been made free from doubts (through correct understanding).[22]

Fundamental to Advaita is the message that ultimately there is no other shore, no bridge, and no path. The Reality is not to be attained for it is already attained and present, here and now. To realize this is to be liberated. Thus, silence is the best conceivable means to convey this wisdom. All else will only increase one's illusion an delusion. Silence, not because there is no answer, but because there is no question. Silence is eloquent because it exactly characterizes the Reality.

All of these are appropriate methods which the Scripture employs in order to enable an individual to remove the ignorance which conceals the ever-present Reality. However, technically speaking, religious discourse as such could be said not to reveal the Reality since the Reality is self-luminous. And yet, if religious discourse is the only source of knowledge per the Reality, as the Advaitins declare, a seeming contradiction arises. The question is, "is the Reality self-revealed or is it revealed by religious discourse?" This seeming contradiction is explained by noting that the work of religious discourse consists in removing all the false notions superimposed upon the Reality.[23] It is not a change in Reality that is required, but a change in one's standpoint towards oneself and the world.

Epistemologically and ontologically, an analysis made by the Advaitins will reveal two things. First, any source of knowledge, including religious discourse, only functions due to the part played by consciousness. Without the help of consciousness, no source of knowledge is a source of knowledge, while, on the other hand, consciousness does not need the help of any source of knowledge. And second, two conditions are necessary for anything to be an object of knowledge. There must be a pervasion by a mental modification (*vṛtti vyāpyatva*) and there must be a pervasion by objectified knowledge (*phala vyāpyatva*). Yet in regards to the Absolute, there is no objectified knowledge since the Absolute is not subject to objectification.

What this analysis reveals is that the work of religious discourse is negative in that the mental modifications remove the objects superimposed upon the Absolute by ignorance, but that the content of religious discourse, with its purport being the Absolute, is positive. That ignorance exists seems obvious. Generally, to remove ignorance requires knowledge. This removal takes the form of a fragmented mental cognition. Yet religious discourse exists in order to point to a type of mental cognition which is not fragmented (*akhaṇḍārtha vṛtti jñāna*) and in which the mind becomes "no-mind" to use Gauḍapāda's terminology. Once its work is done, it removes itself too, thus leaving the self-luminous Reality "revealed." It is similar to the act of using a thorn to remove a thorn and then discarding both. Thus, the saying, "By the mind alone It is to be perceived," and "That which cannot be thought of by the mind."[24] The *vṛtti vyāpyatva* brings the unknown *Brahman* into contact with the mind thus destroying one's ignorance concerning *Brahman*. However, note that this does not help to reveal *Brahman*. *Brahman* is self-luminous. It doesn't take another consciousness to reveal itself and thus though there is no *phala vyāpyatva*, the individual self is identical with *Brahman*.

Generally it is said that the Reality cannot be presented positively as "this" or "that." The Reality is not an object of religious discourse in this sense. However, *Brahman* is understood from the hearing of the Great Sayings (*mahāvākyas*). The apprehending consciousness (*phala*) cannot comprehend an inexpressible-to-words *Brahman*. But the mentation "I am *Brahman*," destroys all ignorance including the apprehending consciousness' attempt to reveal *Brahman*. Thus, all mentation ceases and *Brahman* alone remains.

METHODOLOGY

To a great extent, the nature of any philosophical system is determined by its methodology. Though methodological prejudice is not absolute, the means of knowledge usually circumscribes what can be known.[25] Thus, while Descartes is called the father of modern Western philosophy because of his innovation (universal doubt) in the field of metaphysical methodology, it was left to Kant[26] to start the philosophical Copernican revolution with his insight into epistemological methodology.[27] Descartes accurately described the position thus: "The diversity of our opinion is not because some are more reasonable than others, but only because we conduct our thought by different ways, and do not all consider the same things."[28] And of all the ways to approach the Truth, the subjective and the objective may be singled out as the most prominent. The Advaitin makes both a thoroughgoing analysis of the subjective and the objective, as well as a transcendence of the subject and the object by a direct appeal to Facts in order to reveal the metaphysical Reality by means of this enquiry.[29] Advaita Vedānta employs these two ways of approach synthetically in analyzing the Reality which religious discourse presents. Thereby the Reality is revealed as immediate and the Self of all, the Being of beings, and thus beyond the relative conception of subjective and objective, subject and object. Though its epistemology is realistic and its metaphysics idealistic, the purport of Advaita is non-duality. This word "non-duality" does not mean one, nor none. It is a concept which expresses that which has no opposite. It is a linguistic convention adopted to convey that which is beyond language and thought. Religious discourse is a methodological tool by means of which Advaita Vedānta will employ to remove the differences of the knower, the known, and knowledge which have been superimposed upon the Absolute through ignorance.

Thus, it was said that religious discourse is a conceptualization of that which is destroyed as soon as it is conceptualized by thought. It seems to both reach its object as well as to miss it. Because both the subject and the object are present in an act of knowledge, a gap exists which cannot be bridged. There is no such thing as knowledge of an object, "as it is," independent of its relation to the knowing subject. Any act of observance changes the object observed. This is a fact which philosophy has long known and even the physical sciences are now coming to recognize. For any knowledge to occur, there must exist the subject-object polarity and it is this very polarity which distorts what is known. Never can the subject get over the gap between itself and the object. The subject cannot keep its subjectivity "out" of the object. And yet this is exactly what religious discourse attempts to achieve. By stating the fact of their Ground, of Being, their dichotomy is overcome.

Identity statements (*mahāvākya*), according to Advaita, are the best examples of this attempt because there is no separation between their meaning and the Reality to which they refer. All other types of statements use words to define objects which may be then grasped by the mind, but in doing so, a gap is opened between the object understood and the meaning created by the word. An object as understood is not the same as the object as it is. Therefore one may say that language both reveals as well as conceals. The uniqueness of religious discourse is that it transcends itself when it refers to the Reality beyond the split between the subject and the object. Language truly becomes religious discourse whenever it facilitates the act of knowing into the state of being.

RELATION OF EPISTEMOLOGY TO METAPHYSICS

The question whether epistemology should be based upon metaphysics or whether metaphysics should be based upon epistemology is an extremely difficult one. In Western philosophy, philosophers like Descartes, Locke, and Kant based metaphysics upon epistemology. Others like Spinoza, Hegel, and Whitehead based epistemology upon metaphysics.[30] In Indian philosophy, with the exception of the Cārvākas, Bauddhas, and Vaiśeṣikas, epistemology has generally been based upon metaphysics for the simple reason that the other schools regarded Scripture as revealed texts which embody a direct experience of Reality. Thus, the nature of Reality, as well as the possibility of knowledge, were revealed by Scripture. The task left to epistemology was to denote the various sources of knowledge (*pramāṇas*), the validity of knowledge, and the problems of truth and error. With this ascertainment, episte-mology could then declare the proper method by which Reality may be known.

However, regardless of the priority of epistemology to metaphysics or vice-versa, that a close relationship between them exists cannot be denied. Any theory of knowledge presupposes certain declared and undeclared metaphysical assumptions, and any metaphysical theory is blind without a sound epistemological methodology. Religious discourse directly comes under the epistemological category of words as knowledge (*śabda pramāṇa*). However, the purport of religious discourse is to reveal the Reality, and the Reality is the subject-matter of metaphysics.[31] Thus, there is a mutual relationship between epistemology and metaphysics and the problems of religious discourse can only be solved with reference to the problems of knowledge (epistemology) and its essential nature or subject-matter (metaphysics). For instance: The place and function of religious discourse in Advaita Vedānta is unique. Ontologically, religious discourse (*śruti*) is unreal. It is an instrument of ignorance which distorts the Reality by dividing and distracting one from one's own true Self. And yet, to the Advaitin, it is the methodological tool by which the Reality is made known. Thus, there is a problem, for, according to the Advaitin, Reality alone is real. It is one and non-dual. So the question arises as to whether words as knowledge (*śabda pramāṇa*) is real or not. If it is real, then the non-duality of *Brahman*, and the central tenet of Advaita will fall. And if it is unreal, then what is revealed by an unreal evidence should also be unreal. This again, is unacceptable to the Advaitin. Still, Advaita accepts the unreality of words as knowledge. And thus Advaita must explain how an unreal epistemological device can be the source for knowledge of a metaphysical Reality.

To make clear this issue it is necessary to distinguish between the ontological status of words as knowledge and its status as a valid source of knowledge. One aspect does not affect the other and the criteria of one is other than the criteria of the other. Knowledge is considered valid if it is unsublatable. As *Brahman* is eternal and immutable, knowledge of *Brahman* as given by words as knowledge will remain unsublatable. Thus, it is not true that what is revealed by an unreal evidence must also be unreal. Numerous instances can be cited which show that a non-real entity can give rise to valid knowledge. For instance, a lion roaring in a dream is an illusory animal, and yet it enables the dreamer to awaken from the dream. Likewise, a snake drawn on a piece of paper is not a real snake, and yet from the perception of this paper-snake, knowledge of a real snake may be obtained. Or again, the cognition of a rope-snake which is not real, can give rise to fear, perspiration, trembling, and so forth, which are real.

Thus, the Advaitin declares that when the final truth of non-duality is realized, Scripture also becomes non-existent then (*yatra vedāḥ avedāḥ*). The Scripture is intended for the individuals who dwell in ignorance. It is meaningful only to such individuals and ceases to exist or have any use for one who is realized.

LANGUAGE AND KNOWLEDGE

Language is a potent instrument for conveying knowledge. It is by means of words that communication takes place. "The Word, imperishable, is the Firstborn of Truth, mother of the *Veda* and hub of immortality."[32] It is the universal and fundamental basis of thought. And thought and language are so intermingled that no separation is possible. Language is the essence of thought. Bhartṛhari said: "There is no cognition without the operation of words; all cognition is permeated by the word. All knowledge is illumined through the words."[33] Language is thus the medium through which all knowledge passes. It is the great mediator. Its function is to conceal as well as to reveal. It is the bridge which mediates between the created and the uncreated.[34] Thus, language is knowledge.[35]

According to Advaita Vedānta, knowledge may be viewed in two aspects: the empirical and the metaphysical. Metaphysically, the fundamental essence of knowledge is Pure Consciousness beyond the relative duality of the knower and the known. It is self-luminous and self-existent. It is the non-relational, non-dual Reality. Empirical or relational knowledge, on the other hand, is an expression of this Pure Consciousness through a mental mode (*antaḥkaraṇa vṛtti*) of a cognizer. This empirical knowledge takes various relational forms according to the nature of the object, that is, internal cognitions (subjective) which are psychological and external sense-perceptions (objective) which are psycho-physical. It is through a synthetic analysis of these subjective and objective forms that the Advaitin will reach the non-dual Absolute, which can be characterized as neither objective nor subjective.

The above analysis is the time-honoured approach that Advaitins propose in the pursuit of the Absolute. Coupled with this approach, I would like to propose that religious discourse can also be approached, not from the high conceptualizations of *Brahman* or *māyā*, but from the solid ground of one's own experience. Instead of an "Idealism" involving transcendental conceptions, this latter approach is neutral in respect to the subject and the object. It could be termed a "radical realism," which begins at the level of the given. It is the direct and immediate experience of what it. Relations, with the subject and the object, emerge only as relations when this experience reviews itself.

The impartite Pure Consciousness appears partite in relational knowledge. This process involves the three distinct forms (*tripuṭī*): the knower (*pramatṛ*), the object known (*prameya*), and the resultant knowledge (*pramiti*). Knowledge exhibits two characteristic features—reference to a self that knows and reference to a reality other than self; and the former is no less of a problem than the latter. In looking for a solution to this problem of the subject and the object, one may question the very presuppositions which positivistic empirical knowledge assumes. Its talk of an empirical world presumes there is a world, that that world is perceivable, and that that world is the Reality. Metaphysics is defined as an enquiry into Reality. The existence of facts, both subjective and objective, have built-in presuppositions regarding the nature of Reality. As P. K. Sundaram said, "The initial assumption that science and philosophy could, in terms of their own criteria of valid knowledge, discover the basic structures of being and reality itself is based on the belief that the objective being has a composition that is not foreign to the subjective being."[36] The Advaitin accepts the view that psychological and psychophysical facts may appear, but questions the metaphysical implications drawn by the empiricists thereby. The Advaitin makes an enquiry into Reality, both from the objective and the subjective viewpoints, always asking for that which is foundational to any given experience. His overriding concern is to discover "that which once known, all other things are known." To discover this, the Advaitin makes an enquiry, both into the subject (*Ātman*)—the knower of religious discourse, and the object (*Brahman*)—the known in religious discourse. These two will be found to be identical, one, and non-dual. The process by which this enquiry takes place is both subjective and objective. Subjectively, it is an examination of the triple stream of experience (*avasthā traya vicāra*) and discrimination of the five sheaths (*pañca koṣa viveka*). This culminates in the subjective insight that the ultimate object and the ultimate subject are one. Objectively, it is an analysis of the world which results in the objective insight that the nature of the ultimate Reality is again, one and non-dual. Thus, in the final analysis, to call *Ātman* the ultimate subject and *Brahman* the ultimate object is to be playing with mere words and concepts. The *Upaniṣads* categorically declare that "*Ātman is Brahman.*"[37] From the absolute point of view, there is only one Absolute—*Brahman/Ātman,* which is one and non-dual.[38] Two ultimates cannot exist alongside each other. Thus, the "really ultimate" must comprise both the subjective and objective expressions of the Ultimate. The position from which one starts the philosophical enquiry is not necessarily the settle conclusion. When the truth of non-duality is realized, all distinctions and descriptions, along with the causes, disappear.

BRAHMAN—ĀTMAN

Religious discourse attempts to reveal the nature of the ultimate Reality. In Advaita Vedānta, this is done by the individual through a methodological synthesis of an objective vision and a subjective one. However, truly speaking, the ultimate Reality is neither objective nor subjective. To reveal this truth, Advaita purports that the individual (*Ātman*) is one with the universal (*Brahman*), here and now. *Ātman* is *Brahman*."[39] This kernel of the Scripture is purported to be contained in the declaration that the individual Self and the Supreme Self are one and identical. This central core is most dramatically revealed in the so-called great sayings (*mahāvākya*) of the *Upaniṣads: Prajñānam brahma,*[40] *ayam ātmā brahma,*[41] *aham brahmāsmi,*[42] and *tat tvam asi.*[43] Each of these great sayings imparts a two-fold knowledge which Śaṅkara seized upon as the key to a proper understanding of the Scripture. Firstly, they remove the deep-seated misconception of each individual that they are finite, bound, imperfect, and mortal beings. They reveal that the true Self of each individual is infinite, ever-free, ever-perfect, and immortal. And second, they remove the deep-rooted misconception that the supreme Reality is remote, unattainable, hidden; they declare that the supreme Reality is the innermost self of all, the self manifest, immediate, and direct. "That *Brahman* is vast, self luminous, inconceivable, subtler than the subtle. That shines forth. That is far beyond what is far, and yet here very near at hand. That is seen here, dwelling in the cave of the heart of conscious beings."[44] Thus, the unattainable becomes the already attained, and the farthest of the far becomes the nearest of the near.

It is the thesis of the Advaitin that there exists an ultimate unity, deep-seated within all subjects and objects. The entire manifold universe ultimately and essentially expresses this unity. Religious discourse, as language, involves the duality of a subject and an object and thus is a literal embodiment of denial of the non-dual Reality. Words cannot embody the Absolute for thought exists by fragmentation. It abstracts the impartite Reality into dissociated parts and then attempts to reassociate them into a reunited whole. Thought cannot exist otherwise, for it would perish due to lack of material. But the Absolute is not a whole inclusive of parts.[45] This is why Śaṅkara firmly denied that Reality could ever be an object of knowledge. "There is no knowing of Reality but only being It."[46] Thought cannot hold the non-dual Reality in its grasp, for unlike the world which is circumscribed by space-time conceptions, Reality is relationless. Objects of thought begin and end in time. But, according to the Advaitin, the test of Reality is that which is unchanging.

Then does it follow that the Reality is non-existent? No, for the Reality cannot be thought away. Though *Brahman* escapes objectification, it does not escape certainty. Nothing is more certain than the fact of one's own existence. It is self-evident, immediate, and direct. No one is able to disbelieve in one's own existence. "A man may doubt of many things, of anything else; but he can never doubt his own being."[47] This is because the very act of doubting would be but an affirmation of one's very existence. "It cannot be proved since it is the basis of all proof and is established prior to all proofs."[48] Thus, it is the irreducible epistemological fact and the foundation of all knowledge. It is from this point that all knowledge begins.

This puts the problem of religious discourse squarely before us. The real is ever-present and yet one doesn't realize it. The entire problem of religious discourse may be reduced to the simple question of "knowing" or "not-knowing." The purpose of religious discourse is to kindle an awakening of this ever-present, already established fact. This it does by utilizing the knowledge that appearances cannot appear independently of a reality which upholds them. *Brahman,* the real, is a universal fact of life and an ever-present reality to each individual therein. Though it cannot be captured by thought, all thought reflects it, and depends upon it. Though its nature is inexpressible, religious discourse suggests it. It is spoken about though it cannot be adequately nor logically comprehended.[49] It is not a mere concept, but is the only absolutely real. It is not a mere nothing, a non-entity, for "even imagined things must have something to stand upon."[50]

The non-dual *Brahman* is suggested by a series of "negations" or "no's": "Not course, not fine, not short, not long . . . "[51] And again as, "Not to be heard, not to be felt."[52] As it is beyond all the relative categories of thought, it is easier spoken of by what it is not, than by what it is. Thus, it is called indeterminate (*nirguṇa*) only to distinguish it from all attributes. *Nirguṇa* means that it transcends the phenomenal realm. It is undefinable and unknowable, meaning that it is too great for words to describe and the finite mind to fathom.[53]

Thus, it is said, "An absolutely pure, utterly differenceless Being is very difficult to conceive in our imagination, that is, due to biological reasons, pictorial and practical."[54] This Reality appears to thought as a bare nothing or a contentless blank. Hegel said, "To be completely free from any determination is just what we mean by nothing."[55] Bradley observed, "I still insist that for thought what is not relative is nothing."[56] The Reality of the Advaitins is so similar to a seeming nothingness, a night in which all cows are black, that Śaṅkara was called a "crypto-Buddhist" is disguise. However, Śaṅkara foresaw this objection and possible misconception for he said: "*Brahman,* free from space, attributes, motion, fruition, and difference, being in the highest sense and without second, seems to the slow of mind no more than non-being."[57]

The Advaitins are hesitant to characterize the Absolute as the One except in the sense of, "it is secondless." As Vācaspati said, "Śaṅkara only denies the many but does not affirm the one."[58] This is due to the fact that, for the Advaitin, Reality is not a mere unity underlying the apparent diversity of the universe. Both unity and diversity are terms relative to each other and have no individual independent existence of their own. Thus, the Reality is called non-dual, *"advaitam."* It is described as "not this, not this" only to point to the fact that there is nothing with which *Brahman* may be compared to. The purpose for which *Brahman* is described negatively should always be kept in mind. Even if a negative definition of Brahman is conceptually the most adequate one possible.

As the logic of *netivāda* does not involve any superimposition, Śaṅkara calls it the best way of speaking about *Brahman*.[59] It should always be remembered that all propositions directly or indirectly refer to *Brahman*, the non-phenomenal ground (*nirviśeṣa-vastu*), which is the only Reality. To misunderstand this would be an attempt to know *Brahman* objectively by merely negating all outer phenomena and bi-polar concepts. Yet the Reality is said to be within each individual.[60] The Reality is not therefore a bare nothing. Nor is it an extra-empirical something which exists solely outside the world of experience. It is, and every aspect of experience, whether on the objective or the subjective side, reflects it.

That which is without is identical with that which is within. Whether one enquires into the source of the universe or whether one enquires into one's own self, the final conclusion is that what appears as the manifold world and what appears as individual souls are but an appearance of the one, non-dual Reality. The quest is the same and the technique is the same. One moves from the grosser appearances to subtler and subtler ones.

Brahman/Ātman are conceived of in two modes. One is the all-inclusive ground of everything or the cosmic (*saprapañca*) view of the Absolute. The other is as the Reality of which everything is but an appearance or the acosmic (*niṣprapañca*) view. The former represents a theistic conception while the latter represents the final Advaita Vedānta position.

BRAHMAN—THE OBJECTIVE VISION

Brahman is the fundamental Reality which presupposes all phenomena, both physical and psychical according to the Advaitin.[61] It is assumed as the foundation of all though it is not a substance in any sense of the word. Words denote things associated with either a certain genus, an act, a quality, or a mode of relation. But *Brahman* does not belong to any genus; it is immutable and thus not subject to action; it is devoid of all attributes; and as it is one and non-dual, it cannot form any relationships.[62] And though all words, all thoughts, and all conceptions fall short of the Absolute, still "whenever we deny something as unreal, we do so with reference to something real."[63] The Advaitin accepts that all phenomenal things change, and that the test of Reality is immutability, and thus they demand that a supersensible Reality as the ground of all also exists. This is because there is demanded the reality of something which does not need the support or help of anything else. Thus, it is that there must be some reality which does not come to be or cease to exist. And it is upon this ground that the whole structure of thought, knowledge, and experience rests. This ground is the Reality supporting all things. It is self-evident, and ever-present in all things and in each individual.[64]

What is the nature of this Reality? According to the Advaitin, it is "One only, without a second."[65] No thought can be satisfied with less than the uncompromising primacy of the One as its ultimate truth. Only a non-dual One can be the unalterably fixed core underlying the universe of changing things. There must be nothing similar to it, nothing dissimilar to it, and it must partake of no internal variety.[66] Reason militates against anything less. "It is different from the phenomenal, the spatial, the temporal, and the sensible."[67]

What is the nature of this one and non-dual *Brahman*? "Consciousness is *Brahman*."[68] Consciousness can assume many forms without endangering its non-duality. Even while being aware of the many, consciousness itself does not cease to be one. Everything is rooted in consciousness. And even after the myriad possible objects are elimanated, consciousness will still remain.

By naming the Absolute as *Brahman*, it takes on an appearance to thought of an absolute object—the only thing worth pursuing in a universe of change. But by declaring that "consciousness is *Brahman*," a radical trans-valuation occurs. One's natural tendency is to move towards the supreme object, the other, a transcendent God. By declaring that *Brahman* is one and non-dual, as well as consciousness, a reversal of thought occurs. Where there is no duality, there is no thinker and no thought; there is no knower and no known.

One's search for the ultimate object becomes a logical impossibility. And as each individual is already a conscious being, there is nothing "outside" or lacking to be gained anew. One need only get rid of the superimpositions which cloud the ever-present consciousness.

> That from which beings are born, that by which, when born, they live, that into which, when dying, they enter, that you should desire to know; that is *Brahman*.[69]

Thus, is revealed one of the major problems connected with religious discourse: Can the Ultimate Reality be known? According to Advaita Vedānta, the Reality is one and non-dual and Pure Consciousness. The text declares: "It is not understood by those who understand. It is understood by those who do not understand."[70] Simply put, *Brahman* is not an object of knowledge. If one thinks that they know *Brahman* (objectively), then they don't know. This is merely conceited ignorance. If one knows that they don't know, then they don't know. This is doubly conceited ignorance. Knowableness is something superimposed upon *Brahman*. Thus, the knowers of *Brahman* consider *Brahman* as unknown. To the realized individual, their knowledge is innocent; thus they don't know that they know. To understand that one understands is to make an object of one's understanding. The awareness of Pure Consciousness does not allow for a second or reflexive awareness. As *Brahman* is one and non-dual, what is there to understand and by whom? It is what it is.

IS THE ABSOLUTE KNOWN OR NOT?

The question may be posed, is the Absolute known or not? If it is known, then it must be the object of a valid means of knowledge, for, according to the Advaitin, the distinctive cause of valid knowledge is proof or evidence.[71] And if it is an object of a valid means of knowledge, then it follows that the Absolute is neither the innermost Reality of all things nor is it self-luminous. Why? The sole function of a valid means of knowledge is to make known what was hitherto unknown. How can a self-luminous self be unknown? As the innermost Reality of everyone, if it is self-luminous, it must surely be known. And yet, if the Absolute cannot be known, then the Scripture will be proven untrue and liberation will be rendered impossible.

Śaṅkara replies to this dilemma, "*Brahman* is not a non-object in an absolute sense."[72] Why? It is the object of the notion of the ego and it is immediately known by everyone. No one says that "I do not exist." To do so would be self-contradictory. Thus, the "I-notion" of everyone proves that *Brahman* is not unknown entirely. This "I" will be revealed as the innermost self of all and self-luminous by a proper analysis.

In connection with this dilemma, the Advaitin points out that even though all knowledge of the myriad things of the world comes through some means of valid knowledge, a means functions as a means only through the help of consciousness. This consciousness is presupposed in all acts of knowing and it is the basis of all knowledge. It is only indirectly that all objects are established through a means of knowledge. They are established directly through consciousness. And consciousness is self-established. "Everything shines only after that shining light."[73] Even as a light is needed to reveal objects in a dark room but no further light is needed to reveal the light itself, so, too, is consciousness self-luminous and self-established.

The question whether *Brahman* may be known or not has been posed in another way.[74] If *Brahman* is already known, then one need not enquire into it. And conversely, if *Brahman* is not known, then one cannot enter into such an enquiry. Again Śaṅkara replies, "*Brahman* is known."[75] Not only from the etymological derivation but also because of the fact of it being the self of all, everyone feels that they exist and no one feels that they do not exist. Then why should one enquire into the already known? Because, though it is known as the self of all things, its nature is not fully understood. Some hold the self to be the body, others take it to be the mind or a void, and so forth. Thus, the necessity for a deliberation on *Brahman*.

If one says that *Brahman* is known, the question may be asked: Does *Brahman* know itself or is it known by some other object? Obviously it cannot know itself for one and the same entity cannot, at the same time, be both the subject and the object of knowledge. The knower is other than the known. If the knower becomes the known, then it ceases to be the knower, and by definition, becomes the known. And if one says that *Brahman* is known by some other object, this is impossible for all things other than *Brahman* are insentient and therefore can know nothing. Then does it follow that *Brahman* is unknown? This would have the disastrous consequences of rendering release impossible. Also, as *Brahman* is eternally immediate and the innermost self of all, it cannot be logically unknown. Thus, the *Kena Upaniṣad* says, "That (*Brahman*) is surely different from the known; and again, It is above the unknown."[76] This has the two-fold effect of asserting that It is not to be rejected (all known things are to be rejected as other than *Brahman*) and that It is not something to be obtained (only unknown things can be newly obtained). As *Brahman* is not an object to be acquired or rejected, one's search for the Absolute can theoretically stop. The inmost self of all alone meets this description.

The Scripture does not seek to establish the Absolute as an entity referable objectively by the word "this."[77] *Brahman* is not described as such and such. Its aim is to remove the ignorance which imagines and superimposes on the Absolute, differences. Knowledge of *Brahman* is but the cessation of identification with extraneous things.[78] *Brahman* is said to be known from the knowledge which arises from hearing the great sayings of the *Upaniṣads*. Yet this *Brahman* is said to be inexpressible and unknowable because It is not understood by the apprehending consciousness. To explain: "apprehending consciousness" is defined as knowledge with the reflection of consciousness in it. When knowledge of *Brahman* occurs, not only is ignorance destroyed, but also the apprehending consciousness which is included in ignorance and is a product of it. Thus, *Brahman* may be said to be known and yet there is no knower, known, nor knowledge in such a situation. Therefore, the Scripture says, "Through what should one know that owing to which all this is known?"[79] As well, there are the texts, "*Brahman* is known to him to whom It is unknown, while It is unknown to him to whom It is known,"[80] and " . . . you cannot know that which is the knower of knowledge."[81]

ĀTMAN—THE SUBJECTIVE VISION

Pure Consciousness is *Brahman*—one only, without a second. This consciousness was revealed as essentially and fundamentally "consciousness-as" and not "consciousness-of." But this One is not merely an abstract remote entity far removed from life. It ultimately concerns each individual as the immediate and immanent core in the depth of each one's being. *Ātman* is *Brahman*. It is not to be found as an ultimate object, located far away and inaccessible. Though one cannot know the knower, one can become the knower.[82] The movement is from an impersonal object to the personal subject. Thus, the enquiry leads to a search for the *Ātman*, the ultimate subject.

If one has the knowledge that *Brahman*, as the ultimate object, exists, then such knowledge may be said to be indirect knowledge. But when the knowledge dawns that "I am *Brahman*," such knowledge is direct and immediate. The *Ātman* testifies to this fact that the Absolute is not a mentally constructed object nor a transcendent concept, but an ever-present fact. An analysis of the triple-stream of experience (*avasthā traya vicāra*) or of the five sheaths (*pañca koṣa viveka*) will reveal that the Self alone is present throughout.[83] This Self ever accompanies the contents of consciousness and persists even when there are no contents. It is the foundation of all.

Advaita Vedānta adopts an enquiry into the three states of experience to reveal the real nature of the Self. By analyzing life as a whole, and not merely the waking state as most philosophical systems are prone to, Advaita reveals a comprehensive approach. An analysis of the waking state shows that the individual self resides in a physical body and employes its instruments to enjoy the objects of the external world. But the Self is not the non-self. The former is conscious while the latter is inert. The analysis of the dream state reveals that the Self does not really act and is unattached.[84] In dreams the Self appears to interact with a myriad things. But upon waking, it is realized that there were no dream objects and no interaction. And an analysis of the deep-sleep state shows that the Self is relationless. Here there are no distinctions whatsoever. There is no knowing subject nor known objects. There is no within and no without as all empirical distinctions have vanished. Objective consciousness has disappeared though Pure Consciousness remains. Thus, though the three states exist, they and their contents are not persistent. But underlying them and persisting throughout is the Self. The "I" that was there in the waking state, was also there in the dream and deep-sleep states. The states pass and vary, but the underlying consciousness remains the same.

Likewise, an analysis of the five sheaths which cover the Self will reveal that the Self persists in all the five sheaths while they vary and undergo change. This analysis consists in revealing that what is grosser and more external and less pervasive is less real than what is subtler and more internal and more pervasive. Thereby the Self will be revealed as the subtlest, inmost being and therefore the most real. From the physical body, which is the grossest sheath, to the subtlest sheath of enjoyment will be found impermanence and objectification. But the knower of all these is the subtlest, most pervasive of all. The knower cannot be known for then it would become the known ad infinitum. The Self is self-luminous and requires no other source of illumination. It is not an object to be experienced. Thus, when the objective element is removed from the five sheaths, what remains is Pure Consciousness, awareness, the *Ātman.* Even to say that nothing remains after dismissing all objective names and forms, requires a consciousness which witnesses the absence of names and forms. The subtlest of all is this witnessing consciousness which is incapable of being negated.

ĀTMAN IS BRAHMAN

Our search was for the absolute subject and the absolute object. And *Ātman* and *Brahman* were revealed to have the same characteristic of Being, Consciousness, Bliss. Thus, *Ātman* is Brahman. The purely subjective is the purely objective. Truly speaking the conceptions have no meaning wherein the Advaita philosophy reigns in its pristine purity. Yet, this veil of conceptions, which covers and conceals, is not merely useless jargon. If one thinks that one can lift up the veil that covers the Absolute and thereby see the naked Reality, one is mistaken. One would see nothing. Religious discourse is a veil and it is only through and by that veil or methodological tool that the purport of the Scripture may be revealed.

> To reveal in this sense is not to unveil, to lift up the veil, but to "reveal" the veil, to make us aware that what we see and all we can see is the veil, and that it is left to us to "guess"—or, as we would say, to "think"—reality, which is made manifest precisely by the veil which covers it.[85]

"All this is *Brahman*" renders all language or any part of it at one's disposal to indicate the Reality. Anything can be used. However, the fact of the matter is that there are discernable distinctions which can be made between "indicators" and that religious discourse, as in all else, only indicates the Reality in selective aspects. But the claim is being put forward that there are a few statements which directly and cognitively do more than indicate the Reality in some selective aspect.

CHAPTER 6

East and West

Wherefrom words turn back , along with the mind,
without reaching the bliss of Brahman

Taittirīya Upaniṣad

What can't be known, can't be known.

Wittgenstein

INTRODUCTION

Virtually every Indian philosophical system has enquired about, and determined, the nature of language. In the Western philosophical tradition, some philosophers dealt with language and others did not. In recent times, however, the West has placed an emphasis on the philosophy of language and linguistics. In India, on the other hand, linguistic speculation is as old as the *Vedas*.[1] And the later philosophical systems continue this tradition unbroken up to the present day. Each system investigated and investigates in its epistemology such questions as the relation of a word to reality, the different modes of meaning, the process of linguistic knowledge, and the validity and falsity of words as knowledge.

With the exception of the Cārvāka school, each Indian system accepted religious discourse (Scripture—*śabda*) as an aid of one sort or another in arriving at knowledge. The Cārvākas, Vaiśeṣikas, and Buddhists held that perception and/or inferential reasoning exhausts knowledge about reality and thus they denied words as knowledge (*śabda pramāṇa*) as an independent means of valid knowledge (*pramāṇa*). But the Vaiśeṣikas and the Buddhists, unlike the Cārvākas, postulated a utility to religious discourse. Therefore, according to them, religious discourse has a use and can be determined as valid or invalid through the process of perception (or intuition) and/or inference. The remaining schools all postulated that the nature of reality transcends the compass of perception and reason. Thus, they presented words as knowledge as the sole means of acquiring knowledge about that sphere which exists beyond the reach of perception and inference.[2]

To demand of reality that it is knowable only by perception and inference is too narrow a restriction. "The very statement that common experience exhausts reality implies, by placing a limit on it, that the mind has travelled beyond that limit."[3] And if something "beyond" exists, there should be an appropriate means of knowledge for it. This is the function of words as knowledge as postulated by many of the Indian systems.

The nature of religious discourse and its relation to reality has been primarily determined by the metaphysical position proposed by each system. The Nyāya and Vaiśeṣika schools posit a total correspondence between language and reality. Whatever is real, is knowable, and as well, describable in words. The early Buddhists, on the other hand, say that language distorts reality. And the Grammarians hold that not only does language reveal reality but it is reality. The Cārvāka goes to the opposite extreme of saying that religious discourse is mere prattle, invented by deceptive priests to hoodwink and subjugate the masses. Finally, Advaita Vedānta calls it a "methodological device" by which a seeker after truth will be assisted in unveiling the ever-present, immediate reality. From Realism to Idealism, from Pluralism to Absolutism, and from Empiricism to Transcendentalism, most of the possible philosophic positions have been presented by the various Indian philosophical systems.

As noted earlier, Streng presented three possible paradigms of "structures of religious apprehension in Indian thought." These were: the mythical structure, the intuitive structure, and Nāgārjuna's dialectical structure. I will add to this list one more: Advaita's Absolute Language structure. Though Streng would most likely list Advaita's structure under his intuitive structure, I submit that even though there is an Ultimate Reality referent, due to the nature of Advaita's *Brahman,* a fourth possible structure of religious apprehension arises.

Streng provides as two well-known examples of his intuitive structure the *mahāvākyas*: *"tat tvam asi"* and *"aham brahmāsmi."* He labels these as conceptual symbols. They function only as analogies. Certainly this is the time-honored interpretation for the aspirant or the philosopher presenting a systematic analysis. But, and I repeat, but there is also a precedent for presenting these "Great Sayings" in another context and thus another "interpretation."

Both Sureśvara and Dharmarāja have stated that certain religious declarations may be interpreted in a literal and direct manner and not in a secondary, indirect one (such as analogy functions). I will spend more time on this later as it forms the crux of my contention.

Nāgārjuna did not attempt to prove the existence of the reality of *nirvāṇa* or of the Reality (*tattva, tathatā*). Advaita does seek to posit the reality of *Ātman-Brahman.* Yet, both Nāgārjuna and Advaita knew that conceptualization and verbalization go hand in hand. Emptiness or a non-dual Reality cannot be described by definition. Whether using the structures delineated by Streng, or the methods of negation, paradox, and analogy, this is so. Yet, what of the method of "silence?" Or, what happens when the verbal level is transcended? Who is the hearer and what does such a one hear?

According to T. R. V. Murti, two principal traditions may be identified in the Indian philosophical search regarding the nature of language: The Naturalistic tradition and the Brāhmaṇical tradition.[4] The Naturalistic tradition conceives of language as an arbitrary and conventional tool and denies that words as knowledge is a valid means of knowledge. Generally they may be said to hold a nominalistic, positivistic, and sceptical position. This tradition is represented by the Cārvākas and the Buddhists. The Brāhmaṇical tradition has its roots in the *Vedas* and conceives of language as being of a Divine origin.[5] This position is represented by the Sāṅkhya, Yoga, Mīmāṃsā, Vedānta, and Grammarian schools. And midway between these two traditions lies the Jaina and Nyāya-Vaiśeṣika position. Though these latter are empiricists, they accept words as knowledge as an independent means of valid knowledge.[6]

Before the challenge presented by the Naturalistic systems appeared, religious discourse was never philosophically rejected as an authority. Proofs were neither sought nor required. The existence of religious discourse was accepted as axiomatic much in the way that God was for the biblical writers. The presence of the Divine was thought of as an experienced reality and not as an inferred entity. But with the advent of the Naturalistic traditions, a critical attitude arose that demanded proofs for the claims which hitherto went unchallenged. And from this encounter, two main streams of thought originally developed. The Nyāya school attempted to justify the authority of religious discourse as God's word and to prove God's existence on rational grounds. In contrast to this position, the Mīmāṃsakas attempted to prove that religious discourse is eternal, impersonal, and thus free from all possible defects.

Similarly, philosophers in the Western world have long been struggling with the problems created by religious discourse. As well, much of contemporary philosophy in the Western world has been concerned with the problems of language. And the problems of language carry one into epistemology and metaphysics. Religious discourse compounds this concern due to its supposedly unique subject matter. What is the relation of a descriptive term to the Absolute? Is a prescriptive religious assertion stating a fact, fulfilling a wish, or serving some other function altogether? Is religious discourse cognitive or non-cognitive in character? Such questions must be addressed and hopefully intelligibly answered.

Basically the problems of religious discourse fall into one

of two categories: "description" or "prescription."[7] If religious discourse is taken to be descriptive, the problem arises as to what it is referring to, and how. On the other hand, if religious discourse is held to be prescriptive, the question arises as to exactly what function or use does it fulfill. The question may be asked whether religious discourse is presenting and/or asserting facts or is it being used in an entirely different manner for a different purpose altogether?

A basic presupposition of all theistic or dualistic systems is that there exists a gap between the human and the Divine. In order to render religious discourse intelligible, a bridge must be found which will enable these two separate entities to commune with each other. After setting up God as an "other," remote and strange, a link must be found which will somehow tie the physical to the supra-physical and vice versa. However, great philosophical difficulties rise over the construction and implications of this bridge as built by the theistic/dualistic systems.

Perhaps another way of stating the problem inherent in religious discourse would be to enquire into its exact nature. One may enquire whether it is comprised of cognitive assertions of facts or non-cognitive non-assertive statements. The question may be asked of religious statements whether they purport to be factural, formal, and verifiable, or non-factual, pictorial, imaginative, emotive, and non-verifiable, or perhaps somewhere in between these two positions. The cognitive approach demands factural meaningfulness and verifiability (or at least probability) while a non-cognitive approach is concerned with the particular function or use of a statement. And in between these two options lies the semi-cognitive approach (of analogy) trying to forge a happy medium.

The Western world has always had a certain fascination with the physical realm. This is demonstrable in even a thinker like Kant who couldn't resist importing the distinctions of the world into the region of things-in-themselves. Furthermore, it is not that the Advaitin declares that the world does not exist. The world is there, but, at the highest ontological level, there is no distinction or determinateness whatsoever.

The Western approach generally accepts that the world is there and that one must become free from it. The distinction is real. But, according to the Advaitin, it is this very belief in distinctions which is the root of the problem. Both approaches look for a solution to the problem. The Absolute, Reality, or God becomes the goal towards which the finite individual strives. The goal is determined by the approach to be followed.

PART ONE

Cārvākas

The Cārvāka school posed the same challenge to religious discourse in India as the Logical Positivists did to religious discourse in the West. They held that empirical observation or sense-perception is the only valid means of knowledge. Whatever cannot be verified by means of sense-perception must be held as doubtful and therefore unreliable as valid knowledge. The verifiability theory of meaning demands of a factual assertion that it be open to verification and/or falsification by empirical observation. All the other means of knowledge are rejected as mere examples of guesswork. The knowledge which inference gives is inconclusive as it is based on an invariable relation between the middle and major terms. Absolute certainty can never be obtained about a universal proposition, which is deduced from particulars. Likewise, words as knowledge must be rejected as it is in need of support from inference and thus partakes of the unreliability of inference.[8]

The Cārvākas claim that there is no logical reason or justification for accepting something simply on the statement of another being (human or Divine). If this were not so, one should accept anything that anyone says regardless of its absurdity or apparent falsity. And to define testimony as the communication of a reliable being is simple a case of inference, for one is inferring the truth of an assertion from the being's character or lack thereof. And as it has previously been shown that inference is lacking in certitude, anything dependent upon it must also lack certitude.

In order for words as knowledge to be firmly established, say the Cārvākas, it must appeal to direct sense-perception. Being true to a purely materialistic position, the Cārvākas posit that an infinite regress will occur if words as knowledge is not grounded in empirical evidence or experience. Until the certainty of direct sense experience is established, one testimony will rest upon another, ad infinitum. Thus, it must be concluded that perception is the only certain and reliable means of knowledge.

The Problem of Verification

Ingrained within the Western tradition's fundamental religious assertions is a belief that they are factual and significant. This appeal to the language of fact rendered religious discourse assertions particularly relevant to linguistic analysis. In the 1920s, Logical Positivism questioned the verifiability of all philosophical statements, including those of religious discourse. Before asking whether a proposition is true or false, they proposed that one must determine whether it is meaningful or not. In order for a proposition to be termed meaningful, that is factual and cognitive, it must be verifiable (at least in principle). A. J. Ayer said,

> We say that a sentence is factually significant to a given person, if, and only if, he knows how to verify the proposition which it purports to express—that is, if he knows what observations would lead him, under certain conditions, to accept the proposition as being true or reject it as being false.[9]

Therefore, the criteria of truth and falsity rest upon empirical observation. By applying this principle to religious statements, Ayer concludes that they are pseudo-concepts and factually meaningless.

> The theist . . . may believe that his experiences are cognitive experiences, but, unless he can formulate his "knowl-

> edge" in propositions that are empirically verifiable, we may be sure that he is deceiving himself. It follows that those philosophers who fill their books with assertions that they intuitively "know" this or that . . . religious "truth" are merely providing material for the psycho-analyst.[10]

He continues, those "statements . . . to which no empirical observation could possibly be relevant, are ruled out as factually meaningless. The emphasis here is on the word "factually." It is not denied that language has other uses besides that of imparting factual information."[11] But it is a mistake to hold that religious discourse factually informs and is literally true in the same way as statements about the ordinary mundane empirical world are true and factual.

Ayer believed, much as Hume did before him that this empiricist criterion is an adequate safeguard against empty talk in philosophy. Religious discourse, which at first glance seems so informative, turns out to be meaningless jargon at the worst and futile struggles to say the logically impossible at the best—or so concludes Ayer.

Verifiability grew from its roots in the linguistic analyst's criterion of meaningfulness. They subjected language to an analysis and derived one of two possible conclusions. Language may be used analytically, in which case no fact or experience whatsoever will have the ability to affect its truth falsity. Being but tautological statements, analytic propositions will be either logically true or logically false solely on the proper use or misuse of the conventions of language and nothing else. Or, on the other hand, if language of making use of synthetic propositions, the truth or falsity of such fact-asserting statements will be dependent upon the extra-linguistic data which they are propounding. To verify such statements, one must test their truth in accord with some relevant experience, either actual or possible.

Analytic statements are tautologies. Being merely a linguistic convention, they are said to be empirically uninformative. "The propositions of logic therefore say nothing."[12] On the other hand, a synthetic statement is capable of asserting all possible "matters of fact." Thus, armed with this criterion of meaningfulness, the linguistic analyst is in a position to declare that if a particular statement fails to meet the logical requirements of these two touchstones, then such a statement may be said to be literally meaningless.

Comment

In contradistinction to a non-cognitive position, traditional theism has always assumed the literal and factual character of its basic utterances. The criterion of verifiability was proposed as one way by which to distinguish factual from non-factual language. However, it is an ironic twist of fate that the challenge of Logical Positivism died a "death of a thousand qualifications"—a charge which it was not slow in attributing to religious discourse itself. A. J. Ayer and the other leading proponents of logical empiricism have so modified their position that today even they would accept the fact that there are many cognitively meaningful statements, both literal and informative, which are neither verifiable nor emotive.

The meaning of a statement is not its method of verification. Before any statement can be verified, it must first be understood. Therefore, meaning precedes verification. Before one can verify "p," one must first understand what "p" means. The statement, "potatoes grow in the ground," must first be understood before it can be verified. And what about the statement, "pass the potatoes"? It is cognitively meaningful, literal and informative, and yet it is neither verifiable nor falsifiable. Meaning is therefore, logically prior to, and distinct from, verification. And it should be noted that while statements are true or false, sentences are meaningful or meaningless and thus an investigation into meaning and verification should not be confused.

Logical Empiricism was, among other things, an attempt to account for logical necessity. This worked well with the analytical statements of logic and mathematics which are true by definition or linguistic convention. But to push for conclusive verification or falsification with regards to synthetic statements, in order for them to be deemed meaningful, was found to be too strong a doctrine. All "p" can never be conclusively verified since it would entail examining all "p"s, past, present, and future which is an impossible task. Likewise the statement, "there is a 'p' somewhere," though it could be verified with a single instantiation, could never be falsified.

The method of verification also had to explain the relation of language to reality. In their efforts to link language in a direct relationship with reality such that there is a correspondence between word and object, they failed to take into account the tremendous variety of words. All words are not either object-words or link-words.[13] Such a criterion, if accepted, not only eliminates as meaningless many metaphysical and religious words, but also eliminates many scientific words as well as common ordinary language terms, too. If a word must stand for an observable object, then such words as: "photon," "spontaneous," "and," and so on must also be declared as meaningless. And this no empiricist would ever agree to.

One of the early difficulties noted in the verifiability principle was the status of the principle itself. The verifiability principle is not able, even in principle, to meet its own criterion. It is but a "fiat" or expression of one's own preferences and biases. Ayer replied to, and denied, the charge that the verifiability principle is an arbitrary, unverifiable dogma in his debate with Father Copleston.[14] However, the crux of the matter is that even if the principle is a definition, as Ayer claims, it must either be susceptible to verification or else it is but another dogma. Or, as John Wisdom said, "The fact is, the verification principle is a metaphysical proposition—a 'smashing' one if I may be permitted the expression."[15]

Another difficulty with the Logical Empiricist's doctrine is their definition of "experience." Meaningful statements must be linked to experience according to the empiricists. Such a criterion would be quite acceptable to everyone except for the narrow definition arbitrarily imposed upon the word experience. To limit the meaning of experience to only those experiences which come through the waking, bodily sense organs is to arbitrarily restrict the meaning of experience.

A similar objection may be raised in regards to the concept of "fact." The Logical Empiricists narrowed the meaning of fact down to a small class of statements containing relevance to actual or possible sense-experiences. But unless it can be shown that this kind of fact is the only kind of fact possible, such a claim is itself of little significance and importance beyond revealing one's own ideas and bias. Certainly the proponents of religious discourse never claimed to be making factual claims about the empirical world as defined by the empiricists. The "facts" of religious discourse are about something else, whatever that something else might be.

Yet even supposing that religious discourse statements were proven to be necessarily false, this does not render them necessarily meaningless. Paradox is a seemingly self-contradictory statement. The logical world of logical empiricism treats paradoxes as examples of linguistic confusion. And yet, as John Wisdom has pointed out,

> The curious thing is that their (paradox) philosophical usefulness depends upon their paradoxicalness and thus upon their falsehood. They are false because they are needed where ordinary language fails . . . "[16]

Instead of being cases of linguistic confusion, in many cases they provide linguistic penetration and insight.

The doctrine of analogical predication was proposed as an attempt to circumvent the problems inexorably inherent in (primary meaning or literal) religious discourse. By propounding a quasi-cognitive position, it attempted to steer between the horns of the dilemma inherent in a wholly cognitive stance and those inherent in a totally non-cognitive one. In his attempt to avoid either anthropomorphism or agnosticism, St. Thomas Aquinas took up a kind of reverent agnosticism.[17] If God was taken to be totally transcendent to the world, no relationship between the two would be possible and it would thus be impossible for an individual to know anything at all about God. On the other hand, if God is held to be immanent in the world, then God and the world would become coextensive and indistinguishable and such a pantheistic position would entail anthropomorphism and the death of theism. Aquinas was aware of the danger of attempting to know the essence of the Divine. "We know what God is not rather than what he is."[18] Thus, Aquinas' doctrine of analogy was proposed merely to indicate and to purify one's concepts concerning the Divine. The gap between the theistic deity and the individual was acknowledged as being too great to be spanned by finite man himself.

Thus, the doctrine of analogy attempted to say that God is partly knowable (as immanent) and partly unknowable (as transcendent). It rests upon the presupposition that there is similitude in relationship, or a comparison between terms which are somehow similar. And it is this trailer or qualifier "somehow" which exposes the defect in the doctrine of analogy. No bridge can span an infinite gap. The qualifier is an attempt at a salvaging explanation which neither salvages nor explains.

The doctrine of analogy presupposes and is dependent upon an assumption that there exists an identical abstractible characteristic present in two widely different entities. When it is applied theologically, it presupposes that man possesses certain abstractible characteristics possessed by God or the Divine. Yet the doctrine of analogy fails to find a way to close the gap which it had previously assumed exists between the finite and the infinite. This task it is not able to perform without contradictions and inconsistencies. In order for the doctrine of analogy to adequately explain religious discourse, it must first presuppose the existence of the Absolute, which itself is one of the major anomalies of religious language. It must presuppose that there are certain structural similarities underlying all beings as well as the Divine. The problem for analogical predication is that it is unable to intelligibly ascertain this ontological structure and to relate it to God and human beings.

Flew's Challenge

Anthony Flew paraphrased John Wisdom's gardener parable in order to illustrate that the problem with religious discourse lies in its unfalsifiability. His version of the parable shows that: "Someone may dissipate his assertion completely without noticing that he has done so. A fine brash hypothesis may thus be killed by inches, the death by a thousand qualifications."[19] Thus, the challenge has shifted from the verifiability to the falsifiability of religious assertions. For a statement to be cognitively meaningful there must exist some conceivable event which would count against that statement. Flew says,

> Suppose . . . we are in doubt as to what someone who gives vent to an utterance is asserting, or suppose that, more radically, we are sceptical as to whether he is really asserting anything at all, one way of trying to understand (or perhaps it will be to expose) his utterance is to attempt to find what he would regard as counting against or as being incompatible with, its truth.[20]

The main thrust of Flew's challenge lies in the fact that if there are no experiences relevant to a statement's verification or falsification, then such language loses any meaning. Such language has "died the death of a thousand qualifications" by slipping from vulnerable truth-statements to secure meaningless jargon.

> Someone tells us that God loves us as a father loves his children. We are reassured. But then we see a child dying of inoperable cancer of the throat. His earthly father is driven frantic in his efforts to help, but his Heavenly Father reveals no obvious sign of concern. Some qualification is made—God's love is "not a merely human love" or it is "an inscrutable love," perhaps—and we realize that such sufferings are quite compatible with the truth of the assertion that "God loves us as a father (but, of course . . .)." We are reassured again. But then perhaps we ask: what is this assurance of God's (appropriately qualified) love worth,

> what is this apparent guarantee really a guarantee against? Just what would have to happen not merely (morally and wrongly) to tempt but also (logically and rightly) to entitle us to say "God does not love us" or even "God does not exist"?[21]

Flew maintained that a believer refuses to admit that any conceivable experience can count against an assertion like "God loves us like a father." Such a statement then becomes not only not true but empty or cognitively meaningless.

Thus, what has come to be called "Flew's challenge" is a challenge as to whether religious discourse is cognitively meaningful or mere empty talk. Is it possible for religious discourse to make meaningful statements which are cognitive, literal, and informative even while remaining unverifiable? The challenge is posed to the believer to state what conceivable conditions will verify and/or falsify their basic religious assertions.

Analysis

The challenge of verification/falsification assumes that a religious discourse assertion is a valid factual assertion if and only if one can specify in non-religious terms what actual or conceivable evidence will count for or against its truth. But why must one accept that religious statements *must* be confirmable or disconfirmable (at least in principle) by factual, empirical, non-religious statements? If physical statements have non-physical consequences (and they do) and ethical statements have non-ethical consequences (and they do), and so forth, then it appears to be unreasonable to make this demand of religious discourse.

Still, within the Advaita Vedānta theory of religious discourse, an interesting response to this challenge occurs. To the enlightened individual, "All this is verily *Brahman*." For such an individual, any term, religious or non-religious, has only one referent—Reality. There is no evidence which counts, or could count, against this claim. All statements are statements of fact—that fact being that there is naught else but the one, non-dual Reality. According to this view's insight, religious discourse is empirically verifiable but not falsifiable. An understanding of Advaita's position that Being is the most radical and fundamental empirical foundation of everything, means that everything has an immediate verification and that nothing can falsify this fact. For one who has eyes to see . . .

On the other hand, to an individual dwelling in ignorance, who does not understand the doctrine of Advaita, everything will seem to be a falsification of religious discourse. However, such an individual, if properly instructed, will be able to say what actual or conceivable state of affairs would verify religious discourse, that is an individual's own personal enlightenment experience.

Ordinary, common everyday language seems to be a falsification of religious discourse as presented by the Advaitin. The former exists in and for the world of duality while the latter expounds non-duality. Or perhaps one could say that the Advaitin's religious discourse is a falsification of ordinary, common everyday language.

But the heart of the matter, which is generally overlooked, is that there is no "other" according to the final Advaita position. Flew's challenge has a certain force and validity behind it only if one is operating within duality. Such a challenge is inapplicable and inappropriate within the Advaita Vedānta worldview. Religious discourse is *sui generis* and its purport is to reveal that which is self-evident. The Reality is the presupposition of all else but it does not presuppose itself. Thus, it is prior to all proofs and the question of verification or falsification does not apply.

Authority

The verifiability criterion asked for empirical observations and challenged one to produce evidence in support of religious discourse claims. But perhaps one of the most widespread replies to such a challenge would be, "religious discourse is valid because we have it on good authority."

The primary source for religious discourse is to be found in the Scripture. And Scripture is either the word of God or of some other reliable authority. Believers make claims and assertions which go far beyond their own firsthand experience because "they have it on good authority." They trust and believe in religious statements confidently because they trust and believe in their source. And to trust in an authority is to propose an alternative to making the necessary tests. By taking a reliable someone's word for it, religious language believers are making an appeal to someone who is supposed to know how things really are.

> We accept authority because we discover some point in the world at which we worship, at which we accept the lordship of something not ourselves. We do not worship authority but we accept authority as defining the worshipful.[22]

An appeal to authority is a universal phenomena. By accepting it, one partakes of the knowledge which has gathered throughout the ages. Not only in the field of religion, but in all fields, authority is appealed to as an authentic source of evidence. That religious statements cannot be proven true in the manner in which scientific propositions can be, does nothing to prove that religious discourse is invalid, false, or spurious. Religious discourse may have its own "reason to be" and it is enough if it consistently adheres to it.

The solution proposed by an appeal to authority holds that all proofs are irrelevant. Those who believe don't need to be convinced, and those who don't believe cannot be convinced. Indeed, any appeal to reason to try and prove logically that religious discourse is valid would be held as absurd. From the point of view of a believer, even the traditional "theistic proofs" are irrelevant. They are concerned with the "God of Abraham, God of Isaac, God of Jacob, not of the philosophers and scholars."[23]

Authority may be approached from two radically different standpoints. To borrow from the Christian paradigm, one approach is the "propositional conception" of religious discourse, and the other is the "non-propositional view." The former conceives of religious discourse as a body of truths that are expressed in propositions. It conceives of these propositions as divinely authenticated truths communicated to humanity by God. Thus, an unquestioning obedient acceptance of these truths naturally follows for the believer. Once one has accepted that God is the revealer of these statements, it logically follows that one would accept the content therein as true. Thus, the essential element of the propositional view of religious discourse is the claim that religious discourse is a record of divine and not merely human statements.

The non-propositional view of religious discourse holds that religious discourse is not a set of revealed truths about God, given by God, but human attempts to understand humanity's experiences of the Divine acting in human history. This view accepts that God appears within the human orbit even while upholding the individual's autonomy. The Divine establishes a link of kinship by acting in a manner similar to individuals and as well ascends into super-human heights in order to guide, inspire, and influence. This approach, unlike the propositional conception, not so much invokes an unquestioning obedient acceptance but involves an individual's voluntary recognition or rejection of God's activity in human history. It consists in interpreting events and experiences in a special way. Instead of religious discourse being the Word of God, it is conceived of as a witness to God. Insight and assent are essential elements to the believer's evidence.

Generally it is the propositional view of religious discourse that is presupposed by adherents as well as critics when authority is appealed to. Thus, the main criticism usually takes the form of, "you are believing in propositions upon insufficient evidence." The main defense hinges upon one's faith "that they have it on good authority."

Comment

Almost all religious traditions rely heavily upon an appeal to authority. The majority of the common experiences of life are beyond one's own immediate experience, and are known, at least initially, from a reliable source. The meanings of words are invariably learnt from others and one's knowledge commences with the acceptance of these early authorities. The acceptance of an authority allows one to assert and assent to things which are beyond one's firsthand ability to verify. It allows for odd, oblique, figurative language to be accepted as valid without making any tests. "Having it on good authority, because they know what they are talking about," thus becomes a viable alternative to establishing validity through verification. The words of religious discourse as spoken by an authority are held to be, in the final analysis, attempts to express what no words can express. Language qua language can never convey the meaning and truth of the divine it is claimed. It is only by faith and obedience that meaning and truth will emerge out of the meaningless and the false. The gift of grace, which bestows understanding, is the key and not the words themselves. Thus, it is faith and the grace which it brings that gives meaning to religious discourse and analysis of any sort is but a futile attempt to do the impossible.

However, there are a number of problems with the proposed solution of trust and obedience to authority. First, how can one choose an authority without being an authority oneself? For this choice to be reasonable and not whimsical, it must be based upon supportable grounds. How does one know that this authority knows correctly and thus is worth relying upon?. To know whether the authority knows or not implies that one also knows something about this subject. And yet, how can one know anything beforehand if one's only source of knowledge about this something can come from an authority?

What are the tests to establish if one is an authority or not? In regards to mundane, empirical matters one can always appeal to what the authority can do. One can always taste a cook's food or observe a gardener's prize-winning flowers. But what constitutes an authority on religion? A charismatic personality, humility, authoritativeness, and so forth, are no guarantee of one being an authority.

A second objection rises in regards to trusting in something that one doesn't understand. If religious language cannot be understood except on faith and trust, then one must be believing in something which quite possibly could turn out to be nothing. There is no guarantee that the authority is not misleading one. If there is no independent way of checking on the validity of what is being propounded, one is consenting to any and everything if one declares their faith in it. If one doesn't know what it is that one is trusting in, and yet one avows faith in it, it follows that anything is theoretically possible.

There must be some semblance of meaning and truth in religious discourse qua religious discourse or else there would be no difference between religious discourse and any other type of language. If all language is false and meaningless and only by the grace of God meaning and truth can be conveyed, then the meaningless words of Scripture would be like any other words. If God can use a grocery shopping list to convey truth and meaning of the divine, then why respect or believe in Scripture any more than a mere shopping list? The nature of religious discourse is not totally irrational or without relevance if it is conceded that it somehow points to or reveals the divine better than other types of language.

A final difficulty arises from the fact that if it is granted that the truth and meaning of Scripture comes "from without," or from God, then there is no possible right for one to reject anyone's claim to their own Scripture. Without a criteria to reject as inappropriate the claims of each and every dispensation, is to open the door for every imposter and zealot, fanatic and lunatic. As H. J. Paton said, "To declare war upon reason is to alienate all who care for truth and to hold open the door for the imposter and the zealot."[24]

Nāgārjuna

Nāgārjuna denied any external referent in language whatsoever. Language, he claimed, arises from and serves the needs of deluded existence as interpreted by the intellect. Words appear to refer to entities, but, in fact, are nothing more than handy labels for dealing with practical situations.

This extreme position, coupled with Nāgārjuna's refusal to view the Void/Emptiness/Transparency (*śūnya*) as the ground of the relative, has a number of damaging consequences. Firstly, the *śūnya* is so removed from the relative that it does not touch one's life at any point whatsoever. To be so transcendent appears to all consideration as exactly what is meant by a mere nothing.

Both Advaita and Nāgārjuna agree on the doctrine of non-origination (*ajātivāda*). They differ in that Advaita bases its claims on Scriptural grounds and then supports its conclusions by independent reasoning. Nāgārjuna's theory is based solely on the logic of his four-cornered negation (*prāsaṅgika*).

Thus, Nāgārjuna and Advaita, agree only to disagree. Nāgārjuna concludes that the phenomenal universe is nothing but a meaningless chaos of momentary sensations. Buddha's silence led to momentariness based upon Nothing establishing an absolute negativism. While the doctrine of Advaita employs the contradictions inherent in the empirical universe to point to the Absolute as the only real existent.

Nāgārjuna argued that the phenomenal world is inexplicable, that is, neither real, unreal, both, nor neither. As well, the Void is also inexplicable. The Advaitin claims that this dual inexplicability cuts the root of comparability or distinction between the two. For something to be true and real or false and unreal, there must be a basis or ground upon which this comparison can be made. Yet, Nāgārjuna declares that all is Void.

The same objection can be made in another way. Nāgārjuna posits that there are two truths. And at the same time, he posits that there is no reality. If this is so, how does he make a distinction between the two truths? Appearance has a meaning only if there is a Reality admitted. Without a criterion which can effect a difference between phenomenal reality and absolute reality, how can this distinction be conceived of, let alone made?

Advaita can make this distinction because it posits *Brahman* or the Absolute as the Reality of which the phenomenal world is an appearance. There are not two truths, but only one of which the phenomenal is an appearance. On its own, the phenomenal has no substance and is reducible to the Absolute. The unreal world can be spoken of because it has as its ground the real Absolute.

A case may be made to interpret Nāgārjuna's *śūnya,* not as Void/Nothingness but as *Brahman.* This position posits that the term "void" is used because the Reality appears as nothing from an empirical standpoint. To the mind, the Reality is inconceivable and a total denial of all names and forms.

Thus, to say that nothing is born and nothing dies may be construed as saying that the origination of all things is but an appearance. Since all things are, in reality, the Absolute, which is eternal, nothing is born and nothing does die. The Self alone is.

However, be it noted, that this interpretation of Nāgārjuna, though possible, is not accepted by Buddhists themselves.

PŪRVA MĪMĀṂSĀ

Words as Knowledge Defined

"Words as knowledge" (*śabda pramāṇa*) is defined as the "cognition of something not present to the senses, produced by the knowledge of words." It is thus the cognition of things imperceptible. And it may derive from words uttered by human beings or it may spring from the *Vedas.*[25] The former is considered valid only if it comes from a trustworthy source, while the latter is considered eternally self-valid. "A cognition brought about by Vedic injunctions cannot be set aside at any time or place or under any conditions."[26]

Regarding human utterances, there is a difference of opinion between Prabhākara and Kumārila, The former holds that non-Vedic verbal cognition can only be a type of inference.[27] He holds that such statements are obviously not self-valid and that they depend upon an unquestionable authority for their validity. Their validity is established only indirectly. But Kumārila, on the other hand, considers such statements as a valid means of knowledge so long as their authors are trustworthy. Thus, Kumārila divides words as knowledge into human (*pauruṣeya*) and impersonal (*apauruṣeya*), and both types are regarded by him as valid.

Ritualistic Pragmaticism

The *Pūrva-mīmāṃsā-sūtra* of Jaimini commences with the aim of investigating and ascertaining the nature of religious duty (*dharma*).[28] As religious duty is not a physical entity, it cannot be known through perception or any of the other means of valid knowledge that presupposes the work of perception. Thus, Jaimini concludes that religious duty is knowable only through the Scripture. And the essence of the Scripture is injunctions and commandments that tell what ought to be done (*vidhi*) and what ought not to be done (*niṣedha*), according to him.

The be all and end all of Scripture is ritual injunctions, according to the Mīmāṃsakas. "Other texts are authoritative only in so far as they help the individual to action."[29] Thus, any descriptive information, which may occur in the Scripture, derives its meaningfulness only from the imperative statements herein. By themselves, existential statements are meaningless and have no independent logical status. It is only as complements of injunctions that they gain meaning, for the Scripture need not say anything about an existent entity (as such things can readily be perceived and are not therefore in need of the Scripture). The Scripture is there to point out the goal and to describe how to reach it. Its purpose is to inform individuals about what one should and should not do. Knowledge of existential things is in no way conducive to this end. Therefore, the Mīmāṃsakas contend that action alone will lead one to heaven and for this purpose the Scripture exists.

The Mīmāṃsakas seek to justify their position that language is action-oriented by a theory of learning that posits that the meanings of words are learnt only in the context of actions. A child hears certain commands and observes the actions which accompany them. By a process of insertion and elimination, the child understands the meaning of the words involved. Thus, words become meaningful only when they are associated with commands. An existential or assertive statement is auxiliary to injunctive sentences. The verb is the principal part of speech in an injunctive sentence and nouns, adjectives, and so forth, are to be understood only as modifying the verb. And, in the verb, the injunctive suffix is the most important factor. It signifies what-is-to-be-done (*niyoga*). Thus, the Scripture teaches primarily activity and what prompts this activity is the cognition of a command.

Authority of Veda

The Mīmāṃsakas main objective is to establish that Scripture is infallibly authoritative. They would like to prove that religious language is a valid means of communication of the greatest import. To do this they begin by postulating that all knowledge is self-valid; both in respect of its origin and in respect to its ascertainment.[30] The causes which give rise to knowledge themselves account for its validity. And likewise, when the knowledge is known, its truth is also known. Thus, the validity of knowledge is intrinsic, as well as self-evident. All knowledge is presumed valid and one need not ask why. It is only when there is a failure of knowledge that one should seek its cause. If knowledge proves to be invalid, its invalidity will be due to the presence of some adventitious defect. Thus, truth is natural to knowledge and error is something unnatural, which occurs when there is a defect in the instrument of knowledge.

This theory of the self-validity of knowledge means that the authority of Scripture is immune from invalidity. Why? Neither the external circumstances that render knowledge invalid nor the means of discovering contradictory and conflicting knowledge exist in the case of Scripture. This is so because the Mīmāṃsakas hold a theory that the *Veda* is self-existent, eternal, and without an author (human or Divine).[31]

Thus, there can be flaw in its source. Likewise, words as knowledge cannot be contradicted by perception or any other means of knowledge based upon perception because what Scripture refers to relates only to the supersensuous and therefore is empirically unknowable. That the *Veda* has no author has been elaborately argued on such grounds that if there had been any author, his name would have been known and remembered. And the eternality of the *Veda* is sought to be established by a certain philological theory. This latter view requires further elucidation. The Mīmāṃsakas lay great stress upon the claim that the relationship between a word and its meaning is natural and not created by convention. That is, independent of any entity, human or Divine, there is a necessary and eternal relationship between a word and its meaning. A word is only an aggregate of letters and a clear distinction is made between (*varṇa*) and their tone or mode of utterance (*dhvani*). A letter is an articulate sound conceived of as partless, omnipresent, and eternal.[32] A letter can be uttered several times, or in several ways—yet these are but incidents of accidental features which in no way alter the eternal, changeless letter. The letter "a," for instance, may be uttered in various tones and in several ways, but yet it is the sound. The variety of ways in which a sound is uttered is due to differences in the means of utterance. And two or more letters make up a word that expresses an eternal universal. This logically follows, for letters are eternal, words are eternal, and universals are eternal, and thus the relationship between them will be eternal.

However, this eternal relationship between a word and its meaning, even if granted, does not establish that the *Veda* alone is eternal. The eternality of words merely serves as a negative argument to preclude the conclusion that whatever consists of words must have had an origin in time. If the eternality of words and their meanings constituted the criterion that the *Veda* is eternal, then all literary words and all uttered statements likewise would be eternal. But the Mīmāṃsakas contend that it is a unique feature which the *Veda* alone possesses that gives it the distinction of being eternal. This feature is the particular order in which the words occur in the *Veda*. No author, human or Divine, has arranged these words in this order. The *Veda* alone, and not other literary works, is considered to be eternal because the order in which its words occur is permanent.[33] "The *Veda* has been preserved intact during a beginningless period by being handed down from teacher to pupil with scrupulous care."[34]

Historically, fundamental religious statements have been believed to be not only cognitive but also true. The Western tradition generally holds that there are religious realities which are factually valid. A cognitive statement is one which is factual, informative, and either true or false. A non-cognitive statement, on the other hand, is neither true nor false. Their purpose is other than to describe facts or convey information. "We do not ask of a swearword, or a command, or the baptismal formula, or a sonnet whether it is true."[35] Thus, the question may be asked whether the statements of religious discourse are cognitive or non-cognitive. Can its assertions be determined to be true or false irrespective of the intention or context in which they appear?

A number of theories in the West have arisen which propose, in a manner similar to the Mīmāṃsaka, that religious discourse is non-cognitive. These theories claim that religious discourse is meaningful not because it is cognitive but because it has a *use* or *function*. Thus, the problem of religious discourse is sought to be solved by showing that, though non-factual and non-cognitive, religious assertions still have a function which can be discovered by suitable observations. For instance, besides asserting religious truths, religious discourse fulfills any number of functions such as instructing one to pray, to exhort, to praise, to promise and to obey its commandments. Religious discourse enables a believer to do various activities which form part of one's religious life. Besides making factual, informative claims, religious discourse achieves things by means of what may be termed its "effective" side. The various non-cognitive accounts of religious discourse attempt to find meaning within religious statements by showing that they have a use and that that use can be discovered by suitable observations and stated in straightforward propositions.

Analysis

The non-cognitive theories claim that religious discourse is meaningful, not because it is asserting valid facts, but because it has a use or function. Their position is basically a weak form of the Mīmāṃsaka's position. Though the Mīmāṃsaka thinks that religious discourse is true and valid due to their special conception of the *Veda*, their main thrust is to show that Scripture is authoritative only in so far as they help an individual to action. "Action-orientation" is thus a common feature of these two positions.

The Advaita position in regards to action is well-known. Action generally produces a change of some sort and this is unthinkable with regards to the Absolute. There do exist scriptural texts that give information about the Reality and are in no sense connected with action. Given the conditions, an established fact does not require action to validate it. It is what it is. Whether someone does something about or doesn't do something about it is the individual's perogative. But the fact itself merely gives information. And information can be meaningful without an act. Further, it should be noted that knowledge itself is not a mental activity.

Thus, there is the text, "that thou art." It propounds that the individual soul *is* the Reality. There is no necessity to think or imagine or meditate this fact. It is a factual, cognitive claim stating what it means. It should not be interpreted as a symbol or a metaphor. If it were a symbolic statement then the understanding of its meaning would not destroy one's ignorance and facilitate liberation.

Cognitive scriptural statements are meaningful whether they are put to a use or not. A factual statement has its own meaning and this is not dependent upon whether the object that it denotes is put to a use or not. That it can be put to a use is a subsequent matter and does not affect the knowledge itself.

The other way to meet Flew's challenge is to approach it head on. Basil Mitchell,[36] John Hick,[37] and W. F. Zuurdeeg[38] claim that there are central religious statements which are statements of fact, and which are therefore verifiable or falsifiable at least in principle. But the problem these solutions run into is that either their solutions slide towards an anthropomorphic referent and thereby become philosophically and religiously unacceptable or when the solution refers to a non-anthropomorphic referent, the language becomes obscure and no one really knows what one is talking about. Such solutions are persuasive and one can learn to talk this way, but a true solution as to what religious language is meaning will still be elusive.

Ian T. Ramsey's[39] contention, as well as H. H. Price's,[40] are in many ways compatible with features in Advaita Vedānta. But where the former solutions slip into difficulty is that they are not able to bridge the gap between individuals and the Reality. And without the foundation being stable, such insights lose their credibility in the final resort. Religious discourse does take place in a context, and personal effort is required in understanding its meaning. All that is left to be required is to fix the ground in which it will all make sense.

Even if it is granted that religious discourse is about a "mystery," (*Deus Absconditus/Mysterium Tremendium*), still in order for religious discourse to be at all intelligible it must somehow be understandable by those who encounter it. According to Advaita, reason is not a means of establishing the Absolute, but it is an aid. And even there, it is not an aid to the Scripture directly but only indicates the direction in which to look. Its function is to eliminate ignorance.

It is obvious that not all of religious discourse statements are equally authoritative. It is claimed that only purportful Scripture is authoritative. And in order to determine the purport of scriptural statements, the Advaitin employs the six marks (*ṣaḍliṅga*) of which one is "intelligibility in the light of reasoning" (*upapatti*).

Reason is obviously not a competent instrument for the

comprehension of the non-dual Reality. But it is helpful in the following ways. It is needed to determine which is the initial and which the concluding passages as well as to determine their harmony. It is needed to determine whether an implied meaning is intended, and if so, which type. It is needed to apply the four marks of *ākāṇkṣā, yogyatā, āsatti, tātparya.* It is needed to distinguish the eternal from the non-eternal. It is needed even to criticize itself. Without the work of reason, the purport of the *mahāvākyas* would not arise and there would be no liberation. Still, by itself, liberation will not arise. It needs the help of the *mahāvākyas.* In fact, by itself reason may prove anything at all.

Thus, Advaita's use of scriptural authority is not dogmatic: Reason is ancillary to, and supportive of, religious discourse. The Advaita Vedānta school takes its stand of Scripture and then makes use of reasoning to show how Scripture meets the demands of reason. "Even if a hundred scriptural texts declaring fire to be cold or non-luminous will not attain authoritativeness."[41] And again, "That which is accepted or believed in without proper inquiry prevents one from reaching the final good and results in evil consequences."[42]

Advaita culminates in experience. Thus, it is said, *"śruti, yukti, anubhava."* The knowledge that is revealed by Scripture, and is intelligible in the light of reason, must become a matter of direct experience. Only then does Scripture fulfill its purpose.

Comment

The thought of the Advaitins is powerful, ambiguous, and highly elastic. It is powerful in that it sweeps before it every last conceivable idol. It is ambiguous in that its referent is forever and eternally ineffable. It is highly elastic in that it encompasses many directions and resists none. And it is precisely because of these aspects that their thought is open to refutations, misinterpretations, attack, and counterattack.

An objection which could be raised against the Advaita

conception of religious discourse is that it strips the traditional theistic doctrine of all substantive content. To abandon the personal God, the Incarnation(s), rituals and so on as but true and powerful symbols or methodological tools is to abandon the field altogether, or so a protagonist would aver. God would be dead and Being-itself incapable of approach.

One could raise the objection that it does not make any sense to ask what all beings have in common. This contention is that such a search could only yield either an Essence, a definition, or a common predicate. Yet an essence or a definition is but a nonexistent ontological entity, a chemira devoid of name and form. If it was an existent species or genus, an essence or definition must include differentia to distinguish it from all else—and Advaita's Being is all-inclusive.

According to some Advaitins, no symbolic statement can be literally, factually, eternally true. If this is the case, how can such logically uncertain, factually irrelevant statements evoke the Ultimate Transcendent? How can the inauthentic participate in and unlock the secret of the authentic?

Another objection refers to the Advaitin's claim that the Absolute is unconditionally and totally beyond the conceptual sphere. Echoing Kant's dictim of the unknowable, the Ultimate Transcendent cannot be known in and of itself. And if this is the case, and we have no means of ever directly cognizing it, why don't we just get rid of it instead of getting entangled in an impenetrable fog of mysticism playing upon a colourless screen?

Again, to be true to the Advaitin, they say that all things are subsumed by their subjection to a principle more real than all of them. This is the principle of Being which embraces all ontological qualities. Why some symbols are better than others is that they make present the very Being which the ontological concepts seek to grasp. By an analysis of identity-statements, Advaita is in a position to say how much an expression presents "Being-itself."

The Advaitin claims that God or the Absolute does not "exist." They claim that existence is a determinative description, a predicate of a substance, a spatial and temporal term which is inapplicable to the Reality. Existence is meaningful only in an object and if God is an object, then truly God is dead. Śaṅkara was suspected of being an atheist. Paul Tillich said that atheism is the logical outcome of all the theistic attempts to prove the existence of God after having placed him apart as a stranger.

Advaitins must also face the problem which arises in regards to the ontological status of Scripture. If *Brahman* alone is real, then what is the status of Scripture which is said to make known that *Brahman*? If Scripture is real, then the absolute non-duality of *Brahman* falls, and if scripture is unreal, can that which is revealed by an unreal evidence be real? In the empirical world, a liar propounds falsity!

The charge is made that Advaita has little or no use for God (*Īśvara*). At best, God is relegated to an inferior place vis-à-vis *nirguṇa Brahman*. God's place is tentative and provisional. He is necessary only for certain purposes, like a methodological tool.

Again, it may asked of the Advaitin, isn't knowledge a mental activity. If so, then knowledge is "prescriptive" (as the Mīmāṃsakas) and not "descriptive." What about such texts as, "*Ātman* is to be seen, heard, and so forth"? If knowledge is not an activity, then how is it that one speaks of knowing a thing *now*, which was not *previously* known? What is the meaning of such phrases as, "production of knowledge" and "dispelling of ignorance"? What does it mean to forget? Some change appears to be taking place; some activity or process seems to be occuring.

Does *Brahman* know itself or is it known by some other knowing subject? Obviously *Brahman* cannot know itself, for one and the same entity cannot, at the same time, be both a knowing subject and the known object of knowledge. Knowledge implies a duality in which the knower is other than the known. Yet, *Brahman* is said to be non-dual. Thus, the question may be asked, can one say that *Brahman* is known by some other object?

PART TWO

Śabda Pramāṇa According to Advaita Vedānta
Words as Knowledge

Śabda, in its widest sense, means a sound. It denotes both articulate and inarticulate sounds though in the present context it will stand for a symbol expressing meaning.[43] Such symbols are words and this narrower sense indicates that words are a source of knowledge. Words as knowledge is thus: That which is the cause of knowledge through words.[44] Religious discourse comes under the rubric of words as knowledge.

Advaita Vedānta accepts words as knowledge (*śabda pramāṇa*) as an independent source of valid knowledge. It is a declaration in speech or writing which consists of one or more sentences. "That sentence is a means of valid knowledge in which the relation (among the meanings of words) that is the object of its intention is not contradicted by any other means of valid knowledge."[45] As Śaṅkara said, "A means of knowledge is or is not a means according as it leads or does not lead to valid knowledge."[46] And as words as knowledge does lead to valid knowledge independent of perception, inference, and so forth, so far as the object of knowledge is concerned, it must be accepted as an independent means of valid knowledge.

Purport is defined as the capacity to produce a particular knowledge.[47] As a sentence signifies more than its individual parts, not only must the meanings of the individual words be understood, but also the relation among the meanings of the words syntactically conjoined. It is this aspect which distinguishes the process of words as knowledge from that of perception, and so forth, and characterizes it as an independent means of valid knowledge. Thus, valid knowledge is conveyed by language only when there is an immediate apprehension of the leanings of the words of a sentence and their purport is understood, both uncontradicted and unknown by any other means of knowledge.

The Distinctive Character of Verbal Knowledge

The unfamiliar is almost universally conveyed to an individual through language. The world that is accessible to any one through perception is quite limited in scope. Only what is available to the senses, here and now, is open to perception. And inference, being dependent upon perception, is likewise limited. The predominant medium of education is the printed word, that is, books, magazines, newspapers, and so forth, and the spoken word, that is, conversations, radio, television, and so forth. And this knowledge which is conveyed by words as knowledge therein is distinctive. It develops under conditions different from those of perception or inference. Its purport is derived from the comprehension of the relation among the meanings of the words in a sentence.

Thus, there is a distinctive character which distinguishes words as knowledge from perception and inference. When one actually sees a hill on fire, one has perceptual knowledge of the fact. Again, if one sees smoke arising from a hill and infers the co-presence of fire from the knowledge of its invariable concomitance with smoke, which has been gained from previous experience, then one has inferential knowledge of the fact. But the fact that the hill has fire on it may be gained even though one sees neither fire, nor smoke, nor even the hill. It is enough if one hears the statement, "the hill has fire." This verbal knowledge derives from the comprehension of the meanings of the words and their relation. This demonstrates that each of the three processes above must be recognized as independent means of valid knowledge. Thus, the Buddhist and Vaiśeṣika claims that words as knowledge is not an independent means of valid knowledge are fallacious.[48]

An objection may be raised that the validity of words as knowledge rests upon verification by perception or inference in cases in which its veracity is doubted, and thus it doesn't deserve to be called an independent means of knowledge. But this objection is beside the point. The method of verification of any type of knowledge does not produce the knowledge in question. A method of verification only proves or disproves information which has already been obtained. A method is a valid means of knowledge if it conveys some information which is not derived from another source.

Nor is the knowledge which words as knowledge conveys a mere belief. It carries its own conviction without needing proof. Unless there is cause to doubt what one hears or reads, it is generally accepted as reliable. As Montague says, "To hear is to believe."[49] Verification merely confirms the knowledge which has been conveyed, but it is not its actual cause.

Twofold Capacity of Words as Knowledge

The knowledge conveyed by the six traditionally accepted means of valid knowledge falls into two categories: That which relates to the empirical world and that which relates to the trans-sensual reality. All the six sources of knowledge, excepting words as knowledge, relate solely to the empirical world. And of words as knowledge, it also is of two types: That which is personal and conveys knowledge of the sensible, and that which is impersonal and conveys knowledge of the supra-sensible.[51] According to Advaita Vedānta, "A super-sensuous thing is truly known from the Vedic source alone."[52] It is the means by which to illumine the darkness of things unseen.

Words as Knowledge as Only Means of Supersensuous Knowledge

No other means of knowledge, excepting the Scripture, can impart knowledge of supra-sensible facts. Perception is limited to the empirical world. All the things in the phenomenal world possess certain fixed characteristics such as grossness, fineness, and so forth. Name and form are their warp and woof. But the non-dual Absolute is trans-empirical, trans-sensual, and free from all distinctions. Thus, perception cannot reveal it.

Inference presupposes, and is dependent upon, perception. For a valid inferential cognition there must exist the knowledge of an invariable relation between the middle and major terms as well as the middle term must also be perceived as existing in the minor term. Thus, it is obvious that inference, though an independent source of knowledge, is dependent upon perception and therefore, like perception, restricted to the empirical world of sensible objects.

Comparison gives a knowledge of similarity. It presupposes difference or duality and then relates two or more things as being similar. Thus, it cannot give knowledge of the trans-empirical, non-dualistic Absolute. Where no distinctions are possible, comparison cannot function.

Likewise, postulation also presupposes difference. It is an assumption of an explanatory fact from a knowledge of the thing to be explained. Two apparently inconsistent facts are reconciled by assuming an unknown fact in order to account for that which otherwise would be inexplicable. This process presupposes difference between the two apparently inconsistent facts which need explaining. Thus, it follows that postulation cannot reveal knowledge of the trans-sensible, non-dual Absolute. Like comparison, it cannot function without difference.

Non-apprehension is the source of valid knowledge of nonexistence. Thus, by its very definition, it cannot give knowledge of the existent. The trans-sensible, non-dual Absolute is ever-existent. Therefore it follows that non-apprehension cannot reveal the ever-existent Reality.

Secondary Meanings

Besides their primary meanings, words also have implied meanings. When in a given context the primary meaning of a word is found unintelligible, then the word must be understood in a secondary sense.[53] For instance, the sentence, "the hamlet on the Ganges," cannot be interpreted literally and remain meaningful. Villages are not literally "on the water." Thus, the implied meaning, "on the bank of the river," must be supplied to convey the import of the sentence.

Secondary implication has been divided into three kinds: exclusive (*jahallakṣaṇā*), inclusive (*ajahallakṣaṇā*), and quasi-inclusive (*jahad-ajahallakṣaṇā*).[54] Exclusive implication is when the implied meaning of a word or an expression excludes the primary meaning. In this type, the implied meaning is other than, but nonetheless related to, the primary meaning which is completely given up. In the sentence, "the hamlet on the Ganges," the primary meaning of the word "Ganges" is completely given up and the bank, which is related to the river, is implied. Inclusive implication includes the primary meaning in the implied sense. In this type, a meaning is implied which is other than the primary meaning of the word, yet which is related to it with the primary meaning not being given up. In the sentence, "the school works today," the word "school" indicates the members of the school. Thus, the primary sense is maintained and included in the implied meaning. And lastly quasi-inclusive implication is when a part of the primary sense of a word is given up and a part of it is retained. For instance, in the sentence, "this is that Devadatta," the meaning of the word "this" refers to Devadatta as qualified by present time, place, and so forth, and the meaning of the word "that" refers to the same Devadatta as qualified by past time, place, and so forth. The primary meanings of the two terms are incompatible. Thus, in quasi-inclusive implication, part of the meaning of the words "this" and "that," *viz.*, the individual Devadatta, is accepted and the other part of their meanings, *viz.*, "as qualified by temporal and spatial qualifications, and so forth," is rejected. As the relation between a word and its meaning is natural, the meaning of a word is to be obtained from the word itself. If the primary meaning of the words of a sentence prove inadequate for comprehension, then the implied meaning must be adopted. What necessitates this procedure, according to the *Vedāntaparibhāṣā,* is a frustration of the intention of the sentence and not an illogical connection of the words themselves.[55] Intention is defined as "The capacity to produce cognition of a particular thing."[56] This concept is of vital importance to the Advaitin for it is the key to their interpretation of religious language within a two-level theory of language.

CHAPTER 7

Advaita's Solution

> This is fullness; that is fullness;
> From fullness fullness comes.
> When fullness is removed from
> Fullness, fullness still remains.
> *Bṛhadāraṇyaka Upaniṣad* V.1.10

INTRODUCTION

Our search has not been concerned with merely an intellectual solution. This study is not so much an attempt to compare the various proposed solutions to the problem of religious discourse as it is to ferret out if there is something within religious discourse itself which is *sui generis,* legitimate and valid, as well as experiential. Religious discourse purports to disclose a real experience as well as to express a theoretical truth capable of sustaining a logical, coherent analysis. It is an attempt to say something and to say it about something. The basic question concerning religious discourse is with its precise meaning. The dilemma of religious discourse arises as to how this concept is to be intelligibly conveyed. To put it succinctly: *What* is being conveyed and *how*? Supposedly the objective of religious language is to reveal something meaningful. And yet supposedly the subject-matter of most key passages in religious discourse are generally declared to be ineffable and trans-empirical. How can the relational convey the non-relational? How can the empirical convey the trans-empirical? Generally one is tempted to think of the Absolute or God as an invisible something which is beyond the reach of the senses. And if this is the case, how can one be sure that individuals are not deceiving themselves and being led astray by their own language use? Sense experience is the time-honoured means of verifying with certainty, and if this avenue is closed due to the particular nature of the objects in question, perhaps religious discourse is but another example of the "Emperor's New Clothes."

Another way of asking about religious discourse is to question not what sort of language it is, but if any religious discourse is possible at all. The former presupposes some sort of intelligibility while the latter questions its very possibility. The emphasis has thus shifted from asking penultimate questions to the ultimate question. What is the basis for religious discourse as a whole? Are its roots tied to a metaphysical system, a Revelation, a linguistic convention, an empirical experience? What is it within one's experience which has invited these expressions and which purports to convey or communicate something? The question of religious discourse is thus: Is there something within experience which renders religious discourse necessary and in relation to which it makes sense?

Historically, the problem of religious discourse, of answering what is being conveyed and how, has been approached from various angles. The factual, cognitive approach was juxtaposed with the functional, non-cognitive approach in order to facilitate a historical survey. Cognitive discourse revolved around the concept of verification and validity while an analysis of meaning concerned itself with analytic talk about talk. Traditionally, in the preanalytic period, religious discourse was understood to be not only cognitive, but also true. In more recent times, analysts have been more concerned with the function that religious discourse plays. The various questioners enquired into the factuality, validity, intelligibility, meaning, and use of this system of communication. And from this enquiry, two basic alternatives came to be distinguished. Either one could hold that religious discourse statements are not factually informative, or one could maintain that such statements are factually informative but that an empirically established meaning and process of verification need not necessarily apply to them. The former, the non-cognitive approach, attempts to sidestep the problem of verification while the latter, the cognitive approach, meets the problem with its own criterion of verification and definitions of meaning. Placing these two paradigmatic types of solutions in juxtaposition with the solution proposed by Advaita Vedānta reveals certain basic characteristics and their necessary consequences.

TWO APPROACHES TO RELIGIOUS DISCOURSE

There seems to emerge two paradigmatic approaches to the problem of religious discourse. Either religious discourse refers to an "other" and the approach to this remote and foreign "other" is through perception, reasoning, and/or authority, or religious discourse refers to the very constitutive being of anything whatsoever and as such is self-evident and absolutely certain. The former approach is both conceptual and mediate. It takes its ground in logic and/or Revelation wherein the subject and the object are separate and its statements are at best probabilities. A gap, whether large or small, is postulated between the Absolute and the individual. This separation leads to a dualism which is characteristic of all theistic philosophies. In contrast, the latter approach puts an emphasis on both identity and certainty.[1] This approach may be termed experiential and immediate. It is a "radical empiricism." It refers to the Being of all beings which is immediately evident and immanently present therein. As the subject and the object are identical, absolute certainty is self-established.

Is there something within experience which religious discourse refers to and in relation to which it makes philosophical an experiential sense? As long as religious discourse is seen as referring to an "other," difficulties are going to arise in answering this question. Neither speculative thought nor dogma *necessarily* and indubitably are able to cross the gap of duality. It is only in the radical non-duality of the experiencer with the experienced that such statements have a consistent and coherent meaning.

CONSEQUENCES OF THE TWO APPROACHES

One of the consequences of placing God or the Absolute apart is that knowledge thereof must be hypothetical and conjectural. This knowledge is based on an interaction between the observer and the observed. Yet an insurmountable problem arises in that the objectification of the "other" demands neutralization of the subject if this knowledge is to reach certainty as to the true nature of the phenomena. Absolute objectivity demands that the observer's subjectivity be excluded. Yet such an absolute integrity of an observed phenomena cannot be preserved within the domain of logical thought which necessarily demands the observer separate from the observed. Philosophy has recognized this fact for a long time while modern science is just coming to accept it now. "The observed system is required to be isolated in order to be defined, yet interacting in order to be observed."[2] This estrangement makes the Absolute no better than a postulated entity. And if there is no experiential verification forthcoming, then there is little justification for such a metaphysical postulation. On this basis, it would seem that the modern Positivists have a legitimate reason for criticizing speculative metaphysics.

A possible rejoinder to this objection centers on the assumption that metaphysical entities require physical verification. There does not exist any *necessary* reason why this must be so. It is quite within the sphere of possibilities for a realm of metaphysical entities to exist, complete with its own language, logic, and reason to be. Still, if one is looking for the bedrock of certainty, it would behoove one to attempt to satisfy all the challenges that one encounters in a manner acceptable to the challenge. Postulation will never achieve the certainty that personal experience does. And a rejoinder by mere fiat leaves the issue still in doubt.

The Advaitin as well is looking for more than a mere theoretical construct. All of one's epistemological conjectures need to be anchored somewhere. One of the consequential problems that the Western philosophers, as well as their Indian counterparts, have had to face is how to explain or justify knowledge of the "other." While Kant had thought that it was a scandal to philosophy that there was lacking a cogent proof for the reality of the world outside oneself, Heidegger thought the true scandal was not that such a proof was lacking, but that it was even looked for. Pushing further, the Advaitin avers that it is a scandal to even look for a proof for the existence of the Absolute, for objectification creates an insurmountable problem in attempting to preserve a knowledge of the reality of the empirical world independent of the observer. Sense-perception has been found to be unreliable when it comes to understanding the phenomenal world *as-it-is* independent of the knower thereof. For the Advaitin, however, epistemology and metaphysics coalesce in that the Absolute is itself conceived to be of the nature of knowledge. Thus: To know is to be. Since the Absolute of the Advaitin is involved in each and every experience as the experiencer's, as well as the experience's, ground and substantive Being, it is not open to the charge of being but a hypothetical postulate. The Absolute is a fact of direct experience. As long as there exists a distinction between the knower and the known, the object can never be completely known. Therefore absolute knowledge of an ultimate object can never be achieved intellectually. It is only when the knower and the known are identical that certainty can be established. Thus, to the Advaitin, religious discourse is not mere opinion, nor theory, still less an expression of feeling. Instead of being neither true nor false, as the Logical Empiricists might say, religious discourse is composed of statements that communicate that fundamental fact which makes all understanding and knowledge possible. Therefore, religious discourse is both cognitive and true.

A second consequence of placing the Absolute apart as an "other" is that experience is downplayed and reason becomes extolled. Thought was found easier to manipulate than a God in his faraway heaven. In the West, Greek philosophy was primarily based on deductions from some fundamental axiom or principle and not obtained inductively from experience. And from the time of Aristotle, who placed an emphasis on logical thinking, right through the legacy of the Cartesian doubting-demon, which implied that all sense-experiences may be delusory, down to the present Positivistic period, a mechanistic worldview was seen in which reason came to find a predominant place. The mind was extolled and the world was fragmented. The presupposition was that whatever could be said, could be said clearly and succinctly.

Thus, though religious discourse in the dualistic systems seems to have originally been a report of Divine manifestations of an "other" such as Moses,[3] Elijah,[4] Mohammed,[5] and so forth, had, these experiences came to be doubted, reinterpreted, or otherwise explained. The initial experience was reduced to a supreme concept or an Absolute Object and thus ceased to be a living reality and ended up as either an anthropomorphic caricature or a mere abstract idea. The experiential meaning dissipated and thus such statement's significance began to change. Logical thought began to predominate and thus it is understandable when Descartes reasoned that certainty or self-evident truths can only be reached by logical inferences from self-evident premises. Yet, the great defect of this line of reasoning lies in the fact that only analytic or tautological truths are certain. God, as an "other," cannot fulfill this linguistic criterion.

Likewise, in Indian thought, with the passing of the Upaniṣadic Age of Intuition in which the search for truth was interiorized, came the philosophic schools and their growing reliance on reason. Dialectical reasoning and proofs came to be valued more than experience.

Yet rational knowledge is problematical. It is a product of the intellect's ability to discriminate, divide, distinguish, and conceptualize. It lives by quantifying, classifying, and analyzing. And since reason gives only mediate knowledge, it lacks certainty with regards to objects. Its very nature gives it a limited range of applicability. Reason gives but mediate knowledge and mediate knowledge is dependent for its validation upon the validity of some other knowledge which is its ground. Thus, to search for certainty with reason will only lead to a *regressus* ad infinitum.

The Indian theory of inference recognizes a perceptual basis, that is, smoke and fire at some time or other must have been perceived as co-present. As well, the Advaitin classifies perception as immediate knowledge by courtesy only. Perception depends upon sense activity which in turn depends upon consciousness and thus it is not independent. There are so many examples of perceived illusions which occur in perception that absolute certainty in regards to the object perceived is never possible. If perception has been known to betray one upon one occasion, there is no certainty that one is not being betrayed again. Probability is not certainty. Therefore, the Advaitin claims that the immediacy of perception is not true immediacy and that reasoning, which relies upon perception, cannot give rise to certitude.

At least two problems follow from the consequences that experience is downplayed. First, experience is generally equated with sense-experience. Yet the most immediate and certain perception of all, perception of the Self, is not mediated by the senses. In actuality, sense-experience is not as all-encompassing as is sometimes averred. The general opinion is that God or the Absolute does not "appear" as a direct object of experience but manifests itself through a symbol or object, which alone is directly given. Yet Advaita claims that experience qua experience is all-encompassing and it is precisely the Absolute that is a direct object of experience, at all times, even though this fact may not be consciously realized. "The world is an unbroken series of perceptions of *Brahman* and hence nothing else but *Brahman*."[6] Thus, there is at least one entity which religious discourse refers to which is suprasensible though immanently perceptible. And it is obviously fallacious to assert that only what is experienced through the senses can be known to exist. In a dense forest there will be numerous trees which one has neither seen nor touched and yet whose existence one may be quite certain of. If experience is equated with sense-experience, then the question may be asked not only of the appropriateness of concept to content (word to object), but also as to the possibility of mistaken identity. In other words, the possibility of a mistaken personal interpretation can never be totally avoided in regards to the perception of an "other." And this leads one to an even greater problem in that there would be no certain method by which to discover that one is thus mistaken.

The Advaitin places utmost emphasis on experience. Personal experience is the foundation of Advaita Vedānta. *Anubhava,* intuitive experience, is the culmination of knowledge.[7] Nothing can be more direct or intimate than experience of one's own Self. Its certainty is absolute and can never be doubted without a logical contradiction—thus the Cartesian dictum *"cogito ergo sum"* has become *"sum ergo cogito"*—"I am therefore I think." One knows the Self as certain because one is the Self. Sense-experience, on the other hand, is direct only in the sense that the form of the object experienced is non-different from the experiencing intelligence.[8] As objects come and go, their experience may be sublated by subsequent experiences. But that which cannot but remain unsublated is knowledge of one's own Self. Each and every act of perception reveals the Self (even if such a revelation is noticed or not).

Another consequence of placing the Absolute apart as an "other" is that one need then go in search of a proof for the existence of this estranged entity. The theistic religions posited a remoteness between God, the world, and individuals therein. God is thus an "other." God is conceived to be a being, a category within the causal scheme which is sought to be known objectively. All the theistic religions have made of God the Prime Mover, the First Cause, one principle among principles, one being among beings. Then, after setting up the ultimate Reality as an "other," remote and strange, the theistic systems attempted to prove the existence of such an entity. The history of the "proofs for the existence of God" are ample testimony to the futility of such an endeavour. Conceptual arguments from pure reason will never usher in certainty regarding the actual physical existence of anything. As

Kant demonstrated, nothing can be ushered into existence by virtue of formal reasoning alone.

For instance, Anselm's ontological argument presupposes that God is apart and thus stands in need of proof.[9] What is not realized is that this very doubt and the subsequent proof itself are dependent upon the Absolute. Without the Absolute, no doubt and no proof are possible at all. The Reality is a fact of immediate experience on its own authority. Thus, Anselm's argument itself must presuppose a reality whose proof the argument is searching for. The argument contends for the necessity of God's existence whose denial will be self-contradictory. Yet necessity does not belong to things, but only to propositions. Necessity cannot create actuality.

Nor will it help to reformulate the argument, as Descartes did, by asserting that God must exist, placing an emphasis on existence. Existence is not a predicate which adds to the glories of God. As Kant was to say, "A hundred real thalers do not contain the least more coin than a hundred possible thalers."[10] Thus, once a gap has been postulated between God and individuals and argumentative reasoning has been found to lack unconditional certainty, the only alternative left is to introduce a non-rational authority. Then religious discourse is turned into a body of true propositions given to humanity by a supreme Authority simply because it is declared so, by fiat. Once a split between finite individuals and an infinite God has been accepted, nothing but an act of grace from this unique being of unsurpassable grandeur can close the contingent chasm. Yet dogma is nothing but an attempt to base something upon an invisible and uncertain foundation.

It has been seen that the approach of Advaita in regards to religious discourse has not been to disavow experience but to show how it enables one to convey that the individual and the Absolute are one. Tillich said:

> If the word "existential" points to a participation which transcends both subjectivity and objectivity, then man's relation to the gods is rightly called existential. Man cannot speak of the gods in detachment. The moment he tries to do

> so, he has lost the god and has established just one more object within the world of objects. Man can speak of the gods only on the basis of his relation to them.[11]

Any proof implies that one has more confidence in the process of reason (which the proof employs) than in what it must presuppose. The Absolute cannot even be questioned if it did not exist. It is the presupposition, both logically and ontologically, which cannot be denied. Advaita uses ordinary day-to-day language to convey factual information of the highest import. "Religious discourse does not speak about an unknown thing without having recourse to conventional words and their meanings."[12] And the purport of these words reveals that the Absolute is immediately present. As such it is fundamental and prior to proofs which must presuppose it. It can never be denied nor even doubted, for the very act of doubting it is but an affirmation of it. This is not a process of reasoning nor a declaration imposed by an external authority. It is the basis upon which all reasoning and all authorities, all proofs and all doubts, stand. It is the pure experience of which reference to, and awareness of, is always immediate. All else presupposes this Absolute but it does not presuppose its own possibility. It is, pure and simple.

Another consequence of placing the Absolute apart as an "other" is that one's goal is "to know about" and "to relate to" this ultimate object. Quantitative thinking comes to predominate over qualitative thinking. Space becomes dissected and time is unrolled. The spiritual journey becomes an actual movement from here to there. Yet, where does the objectified Absolute dwell? That Being whose center is everywhere and whose circumference is nowhere has no place to live in an objective environment. The problem remains as to how one is to bridge the gap. How is one to know about, an to relate to, an absolute "other"? The closest (objectified) thought could get to itself would be "thought thinking itself." Yet this is a patent absurdity for the subject can never become the object and still remain the subject.

On the other hand, Advaita posits the ultimate goal as

identical with, and being, the Absolute. The goal is not a new acquisition but merely the realization of what eternally is. As such, it is not dependent upon human activity. That which is caused by an action is bound to perish. As the Absolute is ever-existent (by definition), one is what one always has been.

Thus, between the Absolute and human beings there is neither separation nor distance.[13] There is no "other," and thus there is no gap to be bridged. The purport of religious discourse is to reveal this entitative oneness. It is a fact which can be immediately experienced by everyone. It requires no indirect reasoning nor transcendental deductions. It is declared to be an accomplished fact (*siddha vastu*) and anyone who questions it must assume it in order to do the questioning.

The Advaitin is not interested in attempting to prove the existence of the Absolute. The entire thrust of the Advaitin's solution to the problem of religious discourse seeks to go beyond proofs. Anything that can be proven by perception, inference, or words as knowledge, according to Śaṅkara, is limited and therefore unworthy of being declared the Absolute. The Advaitin's position is that the Absolute is a self-established, self-evident fact. "How can that by which all the *pramāṇas* are established, be itself established by the *pramāṇas*?"[14] As the Absolute and the individual are declared to be identical, it is not something outside waiting to be discovered but the very constitutive being of each and every individual, here and now.

It should be noted here that there is a fundamental distinction propounded by Advaita Vedānta. If this is not correctly understood, inappropriate criticisms may arise. Unlike Plato, who regarded temporal entities as existent images of their essential archtypes, or F. H. Bradley who regarded existence as an appearance of reality, or J. E. McTaggart who regarded existence as a species of the real, Advaita regards existence as the essential nature of the Reality. Yet this existence (*Sat*) of the Advaitin is not the existence which is meaningful only in an object. "*Sat*" or Pure Being is not one being among beings. Existence, as it is usually used in philosophical discourse, is a determinative description, a categorical expression. Śaṅkara is quick to point out that the Reality is neither "existent" nor "non-existent" in the ordinary sense of those terms. The Reality merely *IS,* and can never be designated exclusively as this or that. As it is merest Being, no causal relationship can be applied to it. It was by attributing the Reality as one being (even if the greatest) among beings that all theistic systems have found themselves in the inevitable and unenviable position of having to prove the existence of God.

A final consequence is that God as an "other" must necessarily be transcendent, concrete, definite, the source of all things, the active Creator. Its orientation is to difference, to an "otherness." It emphasizes the uniqueness of each being and the difference between them. On the other hand, the Absolute is taken to be general, the presupposition of every being, the universal substratum. Its orientation is to identify; to that which all things have in common.

The problem is an ancient one and basically involves the relationship between the Impersonal Absolute and the Personal God. Sometimes it is held that the former represents the supreme object of human adoration and love. Western Scholastic terminology calls this the" relation between the *ens commune* and the *ens realissimum*." It has also been designated as the way of immanence and the way of transcendence. Both conceptions, however, must be acknowledged to be pointing to the same Reality. According to the Advaitin, whether there are faults in either method, which a philosophical analysis may discover, they both undoubtedly point to the same "something." Assuredly their descriptions and points of view differ. It is the purpose of the Advaitin to show how both perspectives can be understood and appreciated within a context of religious discourse whose content is declared to be the most immediate "thing" of all—the inner Self, and thus is not only abstract but also intimately related to experience. As any experience is dependent upon the Self (consciousness), so the immediacy of any perception is dependent upon the greater immediacy of the inner Self.

TWO LEVELS OF LANGUAGE

These two paradigmatic approaches to religious discourse can both be understood and appreciated within the perspective of Advaita Vedānta. Advaita makes a distinction between the absolute and the relative points of view as a consequence of its epistemological realism. Common sense realism holds that whatever is perceived or experienced is real. The question is whether the object is empirically (or apparently) real or is it absolutely real. Because an empirical object is experienced, some sort of reality must be attributed to it. But, because it is sublatable, it is not considered to be absolutely real. This is the fate of all "others." And yet, all "others" appear only because there is a ground or reality "behind' them. Even as a snake in an illusion cannot appear without the rope where it appears, so, too, the entire world of name and form cannot appear without the Reality supporting it. An appearance implies the real but the real does not imply an appearance. The relation is necessarily one-sided.

However, the real (*siddhānta*) position of the Advaitin is that this two-level theory of reality is a contextual concession to those individuals who still dwell in ignorance. Even the expression "absolutely real" is contextual. Contextual expressions are used with regard to the Absolute for the purpose of distinguishing it from the things of the world. For one who has known the truth however, all such distinctions lose their significance.[15]

Likewise there is a traditional division of language into two levels—that which relates to the empirical world and that which relates to the trans-sensual Reality. Though the *Māṇḍūkya Upaniṣad* gives four levels and the *Vākyapadīya* and the Grammarians likewise state either three or four levels of language.[16] Depending upon various interpretations, it is my contention that there is scope for speaking of a single level of language and that all language points directly and immediately to the Absolute. Such a language could be called "Absolute Language." In order to propound this fact, I will explicate a two-level theory of religious discourse which differs slightly from the traditional one. And then, from this platform,

I will show how a two-level theory of language is also a contextual concession and that in fact, and in actuality, there is only one level of language—an Absolute Language—which then loses any meaning in being labeled one way or another.

Religious discourse was previously described as basically falling into two types or categories. Either it is "descriptive" and states facts or else it is "prescriptive" and advocates actions.[17] Statements that are prescriptions can be distinguished from those which are descriptions of existing states of affairs. For example, statements expressing moral views, commands, injunctions, exhortations, and so forth are prescriptive while statements giving information about the meaning of words, those giving historical facts, and those which are (or seem to be) informative about the way things really are, are descriptive. Nearly all philosophers would admit to this division. As well it would be safe to say that these two types of religious discourse do not necessarily occur in separate places.

In the Indian context these two types of statements are technically called: "injunctive statements" (*vidhi vākyas*) and "existential statements" (*siddhārtha vākyas*). The former consists of injunctions to act. They presuppose the achievement of various sorts of results as well as the recognition of the agent therein. The latter statements are declarations of facts and statements whose subject-matter exists already. And the Upaniṣadic tradition subdivides the existential statements into subsidiary texts (*avāntara vākyas*) and principal texts (*mahāvākyas*)—with the principal texts having the ability to bestow the liberating knowledge of the oneness of the individual with the Absolute.

The injunctive statements and the existential statements have no real logical relation to each other according to Advaita. Both types of statements are no doubt valid within a given context. But what must be clearly kept in mind is the distinct subject-matter of each type of statement. Injunctive statements are valid in regards to actions. Existential statements are valid in regards to facts. Both types of passages tell an individual something which one did not know beforehand and could not have known otherwise. Thus, both types of passages function to make something known. Neither type of passage functions to produce activity. If, upon hearing either type of passage, one is desirous of doing some action, it is the desire that does the prompting and not the statement itself. The aim of the passage is to make something known, though what they make known is entirely different. One may perform an action, may not perform an action, or perform the action differently according to one's whim, but in regards to a fact, there is nothing to be done.

A TWO-LEVEL THEORY OF RELIGIOUS DISCOURSE

The two-level theory of religious discourse I would like to propose is one in which the literal expression, which directly names the fact of the non-dual Absolute, is the first-level and all other language, which in relation to this first-level, is indirect, symbolic, and figurative and comprises the second-level of language. At this stage, all but a few select statements fall into the secondary level of language.

First-level language directly refers to the Absolute (*nirguṇa Brahman*): " . . . indicated by such terms as 'not gross' through a negation of all the distinctions of names, forms, etc. called up by nescience."[18] No meditation or mediation is indicated or required here. The pointing is direct. For example, such statements as *"tat tvam asi," "satyam jñānam anantam brahma,"* or *"aham Brahmāsmi"* point directly to the supreme Reality. On the other hand, second-level language, or figurative language, does not directly refer to the Absolute but points to it indirectly. "That very *Brahman* (the superior *Brahman*) becomes the inferior *Brahman* where it is taught as possessed of some distinct name, form, etc., for the sake of meditation."[19] This proposal for a two-level theory of language stems from an analysis of a unique declaration of Śaṅkara's in his *bhāṣya* on the *Brahmasūtra.*[20] Ordinarily, when the Advaitin is asked if there are two *Brahmans,* the answer is a categorical "no." However, in the fourth chapter of the *Brahmasūtra,* the opponent asks, "Are there then two *Brahmans*—one superior and the other inferior?"[21] The answer is a surprising, "Quite so."[22]

This dialogue occurs in reference to propounding the place in which texts about movement may find proper scope. When the text declares, "The knower of *Brahman*, becomes *Brahman*," the question arises whether this "becoming" or "attaining" indicates movement. Quoting the *Bṛhadāraṇyaka Upaniṣad*[23] to show that no movement is asserted in any way, the Advaitin must then explain the scope and nature of the texts indicating movement. Śaṅkara says that their place is limited to meditating on the inferior *Brahman*:

> Accordingly, movement is possible only in relation to the inferior *Brahman*. That being so, it is only through a failure to distinguish between the superior *Brahman* and inferior *Brahman* that the texts about travelling that refer to the inferior *Brahman* are ascribed to the superior *Brahman*.[24]

Thus, the first move of the Advaitin in regards to religious discourse is to declare that there are two levels in it. At this juncture, their radical stance propounds that first-level language does directly designate the Absolute. As a methodological device it does more than merely indicate. The purport of religious discourse is to deny difference caused by ignorance.[25] Whether the unreal distinctions of duality and difference are removed by denying difference or by affirming identity, the result is that the Absolute is seen to shine in its pristine splendor. Thus, the attainment of, or becoming *Brahman*, is but a "dis-covering." It is the knowledge of one's true nature a one really is. Being eternally attained, where is the need for action?[26]

It is in this connection that the Advaitin makes a distinction between knowledge which is object-dependent (*vastutantra*) and action which is person-dependent (*puruṣatantra*). The former is knowledge of a thing as-it-is. There is nothing to *do* about it. As ignorance about an object disappears, knowledge of it arises on its own accord. On the other hand, the results of action are of four kinds: That which is produced (*utpādyam*), that which is attained (*prāpayam*), that which is modified (*vikāryam*), and that which is purified (*saṃskāryam*).[27] *Brahman,* according to the Advaitin, is the ever-existent immanent Reality of all. It is not produced, for it is eternal. It always is, and has been, and will be one's own true state and thus it is not the attainment of a new state. It is unchanging and thus not subject to modification. It is ever-pure and thus has no impurity to be removed.

Three analogies are put forth to illustrate this "un-covering" of the always existent Absolute. One is about a woman who, forgetting that her necklace is around her neck, goes anxiously in search of it. The second is about a prince who was abandoned in a forest in his infancy and grew up thinking that he was the son of a hunter. The third is about ten rustics who, upon crossing a river, each counted the other nine, and forgetting to count himself, bewailed the fact that one of their party had drowned. In truth, the necklace was never lost, the prince was never not a prince, and the tenth man was never drowned.

The statement, "*Brahmaveda brahmaiva bhavati,*"[28] (the knower of *Brahman* becomes *Brahman*), does not mean a change of state or an attainment. The Sanskrit root *"bhū"* from which *"bhavati"* (becomes) is derived, means both "Being" and "becoming." In the present context it refers to "Being." One is what one always is. To attain the unattained, action is necessary. But to attain the already attained, no action is required. Knowledge of the fact as-it-is will dispel the darkness of ignorance which covers it. First-level language directly declares this ever-existent fact while second-level language does so indirectly.

The opponent then asks whether the non-duality of *Brahman* is compromised if there are two *Brahmans.* The Advaitin answers not so, for the inferior *Brahman* and meditation thereon is confined within the transmigratory state itself—all of which springs from nescience and its continuance. Keeping in mind the Advaitin's contention that there is a distinction between the absolute (*pāramārthika*) and the relative (*vyāvahārika*) levels of reality, no contradiction occurs in this reply. *Brahman* by itself is *nirguṇa,* one and non-dual. But when viewed in relation to the world it is designated as *saguṇa*. Thus, there are not two *Brahmans,* but one and the same *Brahman* in two forms.

To illustrate these two levels of language, let us make an analysis of the two definitions of *Brahman* as given in Advaita Vedānta. *Brahman* is defined in terms of its essential nature as well as the accidental attributes superimposed thereon.[29] *Svarūpa lakṣaṇa* is said to give the essential or substantial definition of *Brahman* and *taṭastha lakṣaṇa* is said to give the accidental or modal definition. Thus, it may be said that the *svarūpa lakṣaṇa* points to the "what" of *Brahman* while *taṭastha lakṣaṇa* posits the "that" of *Brahman*. While the former indicates its essential nature, the latter refers to its accidental nature.

The definition *per accidens* of *Brahman* is from the relative standpoint. An accidental attribute of a thing is a temporal mark which distinguishes it from other things. Such a definition makes the Absolute appear subject to categories and the causal scheme. Advaita calls this level the *"saguṇa Brahman"* or the "traditional God" of the theistic theologies. Such a definition is always open to challenge. The "proofs for the existence of God" are evidence enough to show the tentativeness and uncertainty which accompanies such a view. Reason lacks certainty. And as Kant pointed out, there is no legitimate passage from the sphere of the phenomena to their unconditional ground. The categories cannot transgress their logical limits. Either the unconditional Absolute is within the realm of the phenomena, and thus not unconditional, or else its existence and nature can only be dogmatically asserted.

Still, the Advaitin holds that there is a methodological usage for this second-level language. A beginner will find it easy to understand the nature of *Brahman* when it is defined as the cause and the support of the world. By first superimposing accidental qualities on the Absolute, one is able to progress from the known to the unknown. Then, when logical difficulties arise upon an analysis of categories and causality in regards to their relation to the Absolute, such attributes are slowly withdrawn and *Brahman* comes to be defined in terms of its essential nature.

The essential nature of a thing is present in that thing so long as the thing exists. And according to the Advaitin, the essential nature of *Brahman* is *nirguṇa*—without attributes, one and non-dual. *Ātman* is *Brahman* and thus the essential constitutive Self of one's being. It is self-evident. Everything that is, is. Any attempt to prove it must of necessity already involve a presupposition of it. One cannot even deny it without assuming it. "Since any proof is an objectification of this presupposition, it falsifies it instead of proving it. Hence all proofs should *a priori* fail."[30] Proofs or definitions *per accidens* are indicative of this inherent difficulty.

Categories and causality are methodological aids to assist greater understanding. They are useful and valuable in preparing an individual for the insight that the Absolute is not something far away but is immediate and the very essence of all. Without directly pointing to the Absolute, second-level statements imply the presence of the Absolute as the unconditional foundation of all phenomena.

First-level language directly points to the Absolute. For instance, the *Brahmasūtra* says, "These texts (I am *Brahman*—Br. 1.4.10 and This self is the *Brahman—Mand.* 2) are to be taken in their primary and not secondary sense, as in, The mind is *Brahman—Chan.* 3.18.1, where the text presents the mind as a symbol for contemplation."[31] This means that the self is *Brahman* and that one need not meditate upon the self as *Brahman*. In the text like "the mind is *Brahman*," the meditator is asked to take the mind as a symbol of *Brahman* and then meditate upon it as such. This latter is an example of second-level language, which indirectly points to the Absolute. But there also exist first-level language statements which point directly to the Absolute without enjoining one to meditate upon them as being symbolical of that reality, for example, *"tat tvam asi."*

CAN THE ABSOLUTE BE SIGNIFIED DIRECTLY?

Sentences are said to give knowledge of their meaning through the knowledge of the meanings of the words which constitute them. A word is said to convey a primary signification when its meaning is conveyed through a genus (*jāti*), or quality (*guṇa*), or activity (*kriyā*), or relation (*sambandha*). It is usually claimed that words cannot signify the Absolute directly due to the absence of one of these media therein.

A second reason put forth for maintaining that words cannot signify the Absolute directly is that there is no knowledge of the significative relation between the words and the Absolute. The idea here is that a word can primarily signify an object only when there is the knowledge of the significative relation between the word and the meaning. And this significative relation of a word to its meaning can only be known through perception or some other proof. And further, all of these require comprehension by the mind. But the Absolute is not an external object which can be known through the mind and thus it follows that the Absolute cannot be signified directly.

Thus, an objection may be raised that first-level language must need be interpreted figuratively. But this is to miss the point. It is true that there are some interpreters who do resort to the process of implied meaning to interpret first-level language statements. However, this does not mitigate the fact that the first-level language statements directly refer to the Absolute. The reference is direct even if one philosophically gives them a figurative interpretation. In fact, it is only because one has failed to grasp the literal meaning, that one need resort to a secondary implication at all. There are numerous historical references which set a precedent for such a claim.[32] Even a text like *"satyam jñānam anantam brahma"* directly refers to the Reality. It is only when it is interpreted as an *akhaṇḍārtha vākya* by some philosophers that they resort to a negative method and an indirect analysis to show how three separate words, with three separate dictionary meanings, all refer to the same one and non-dual Reality.

Normally a sentence is held to convey a relation of duality and the meaning of the sentence is conveyed through the relation obtained among the various words comprising it which convey difference. The contention is that a relational sentence cannot give a non-relational meaning. Generally, when two or more words are in grammatical co-ordination, the thing referred to is not different though the meanings of the two words is, that is, blue lotus. When the connotations are different, one usually imagines that the denotations are also different. For instance, "the blue lotus" designates a subject-predicate relation of the qualified an its attribute. Though the two words have different individual meanings, since they are in grammatical co-ordination, the thing referred to is one, that is, lotus. Thus, the sentence connotes a single object. This example refers to a oneness with relation (one flower having a blue color), but there are also statements which reveal perfect identity. In fact, it is just overcoming any idea of difference that is the purpose of an identity statement.

Literally it would seem that the words which comprise an identity statement (*akhaṇḍārtha vākya*) are not synonymous and thus one must resort to some sort of secondary meaning if one wishes to make their statement meaningful. "This is that Devadatta" or *"aham brahmāsmi"* seem to reveal a prima facie absurdity. Yet such need not be the case. The real position of the Advaitin is that there is no need to resort to an implied meaning. In the *Chāndogya Upaniṣad* context in which the statement *"tat tvam asi"* appears, the word *"tat"* does not refer to the omniscient *Īśvara*. It refers to *Brahman*, which is said to be *nirguṇa*. And this *nirguṇa Brahman* is referred to by the word *"sat"* which is attained by the individual in deep sleep, for it is said, "My dear, it is *sat* that is attained." Therefore, in as much as the word *"tat"* occurs in the context of the discussion about *nirguṇa Brahman*, it cannot refer to the *saguṇa Brahman*. The text says, *"tat satyam"* and *Iśvara*, who is associated with nescience, cannot be real (*satya*). So the Upaṇisadic text says, "O Śvetaketu, you, the individual, are that *Brahman*." And how can the individual be *Brahman*? It is said, *"sa ātma"* (that is the Self). It is well known that the individual is the Self, because the Self is the notion of the "I." And *Brahman* is the Self and thus it is tenable to say that the Self is *Brahman*. And this is said directly and without any need to resort to a secondary meaning of the word *"tat"* or *"tvam."*

Sureśvara, in his *Naiṣkarmyasiddhi,* likewise argues that the words "I" and *"Brahman"* are in grammatical co-ordination and tenable to a primary meaning. "The "I" does not exist without the Self; otherwise it will cease to be. And there is no other alternative. Therefore, the Self is denoted by the 'I'-notion."[33]

As a final example, the author of the *Pañcadaśī* replies that the author of the *Vivaraṇa* gloss interpreted "I am *Brahman*" using the *mukya-sāmānādhikaraṇya* because he has taken the "I" in the sense of *kūṭastha-caitanya* and not in the sense of *cidābhāsa.*[34] (See also *Bṛhadāraṇyakopaniṣad-bhāṣyavārtikka* 1.14).

The issue at this stage is to explain how a verbal sense can give a non-verbal meaning and whether, if it can, this sense is a primary or secondary one. When there is a relation of duality, the meaning of a sentence is conveyed through the relation obtained among the words conveying difference. Sentences which convey a relation of non-duality on the other hand, give a unitary, impartite meaning. The claim is that an impartite sentence (*akhaṇḍārtha vākya*) expresses identity even though all the words have their own individual significance. It is my contention that an *akhaṇḍārtha vākya* expresses identity even though all the words have their own individual significance and that this expression directly names the Reality without resorting to the necessity of secondary implication. This is the only way that language, which is usually relational, can give an immediate realization of the impartite Reality. Such statements name the Absolute directly. The knowledge of the entitative oneness of the individual soul with the Absolute is the purport of the *mahāvākyas.* At the two-level theory of language, the *mahāvākyas* directly state the fact of this entitative oneness while all other statements do so only indirectly. At this level, the meaning of the statement is determined by its purport. And for those who cannot render the literal meaning intelligible, the significance should be sought for.

To hear the statement, "someone won the lottery" invokes mediation. A few of the myriad indirect by-lanes the intellect explores include: "Who is that someone?"; "have they been notified?"; "how much did they win?"; and so forth. But when one is told, "you are that someone who has won the lottery," the understanding is direct and immediate. Such a statement presupposes that one has bought a lottery ticket, that that lottery drawing was just recently conducted, and so forth. But given the necessary context, such a statement becomes directly and immediately meaningful. Likewise, with an identity statement, granting the context and preparedness of the individual hearing it, it too will give direct and immediate knowledge.

Some identity statements include: "This is that Devadatta"; "the sun is the most luminous"; "Scott was the author of Waverly"; *"satyam jñānam anantam brahma"*; and *"tat tvam asi."* Though the words are non-synonymous, yet they have the same referent or meaning. This shows that it is possible for a relational sentence to convey a non-relational meaning. In answering the question, "Which is the sun?" it is the identity of the object that is being conveyed and not the relation of luminosity to the sun. In answering the question "What is *Brahman*?" it is the identity of *Brahman* as *satyam, jñānam, anantam,* that is being conveyed. If the question needs a direct definition of what the object is, the answer supplies it. As the question, so the answer.

These examples show that an identity statement can assert a single content. It can do so by either expressing identity or else by giving a definition or description. In the former, one begins with a unique type of tautology. Though the expression, "A is identical with B" (*tat tvam asi*) begins with difference as its starting point, through sublation, knowledge of identity is reached. The existence of a single content is asserted once the accidental and apparent determinants are negated. The "pot-ether" is identical to the "space-ether" and neither determinant (pot or space) affects the identity of the ether. The pot-enclosed ether and the ether outside have the same ontological status. Though they appear to be different, they are not really so.

The second type of identity statement expresses knowledge of a single object by definition or description. Usually a definition or description expresses a relation of one thing to another. But here all the individual words of the sentence refer only to one entity. Whether it be, "the present President of the United States is Clinton" or *"satyam jñānam anantam brahma,"* both expressions convey only identity. Usually *"satyam jñānam anantam brahma"* is interpreted in a secondary sense because the Absolute is considered to be beyond all determinations and attributes. Thus, *satyam* is used to indicate that the Absolute is not unreal; *jñānam* is used to indicate that the Absolute is not unconscious; and *anantam* is used to indicate that it is not finite. But it can be maintained that anyone who understands the *mahāvākyas* will immediately know that *Brahman, satyam, jñānam, anantam* are all referring to the same content. *Brahman* is *satyam* and *jñānam* is *anantam,* and so forth. The text produces the knowledge asked for, *viz.,* "What is *Brahman*?"

Vimuktātman, in his *Iṣṭa Siddhi,* subtly shows how "*satyam, jñānam,* and *anantam*" can be interpreted in a primary and direct sense.[35] The terms are not synonymous and thus there is no repetition. But being non-synonymous, the terms don't indicate diverse attributes either. These non-synonymous terms have an impartite sense. The Absolute alone is, and "*satyam, jñānam,* and *anantam*" are expressions of the same Absolute. They do not express attributes or aspects of the Absolute. They are the Absolute. They do not express attributes or aspects of the Absolute. They are the Absolute. *Sat* is *Brahman. Cit* is *Brahman. Ānanda* is *Brahman. Anantam* is *Brahman.* And *Brahman* is only one, without a second.

As was earlier indicated, within the Advaita tradition there is the method of interpreting the terms: *Satyam, jñānam, anantam, ānandam,* as meaning respectively, absence of non-existence, absence of ignorance, absence of finitude, and absence of pain. But this is merely a ploy to get over the charge of repetition if the terms are synonymous. And if the terms are not synonymous, then these terms become diverse attributes which belies the Advaitin's doctrine of non-duality.

Yet, according to Vimuktātman, such a ploy is not necessary. The terms: *Satyam, jñānam, anantam,* and *ānandam* can be interpreted in their primary meaning. These non-synonymous terms have an impartite sense and thus there is no difficulty involved with the Advaitin's interpretation.

Identity statements are Advaita's answer to the question: Does God or the Absolute exist and if so, can one talk about such meaningfully? History is replete with advice about that which cannot be said: "Words turn back,"[36] "the *Tao* which can be spoken of is not the real *Tao,*"[37] Buddha's and Jesus' silence, and so forth. But this is not to then imply that there is a wordless meaning. Speaking about the unspeakable is to employ expressions. To be caught up in a search for a wordless meaning behind the expression would only result in a futile *regressus* ad infinitum. What is not immediate and direct, will forever lack certainty.

According to Advaita, religious discourse primarily concerns itself with the ontological realm. Its subject-matter is the very constitutive depth of any and everything whatsoever. Obviously the language qua language is not the subject suggested. But neither is it something entirely different either. Unlike the Grammarians who declare that language is the Reality and unlike the theists who declare that never the twain shall meet between God and man, the Advaitins say that religious discourse carries within itself its own revelation. The purpose of religious discourse is to name and/or suggest and certainly it would be a mistake to accept that what names or suggests for what is being named or suggested. However, it would be equally wrong to look for Reality somewhere else. For according to Advaita, in all cognitions the Reality is eternally present and self-manifest. Thus, to perceive language is to perceive the Reality as seemingly delimited by language. For those who dwell in ignorance, language is the Reality appearing as language. And for those who are enlightened, language is the Reality appearing as the Reality. In either case, the Absolute or God is not beyond or behind the language. Language is therefore an instrument of ignorance as well as an instrument for liberation. Any dualistic approach to this problem will only land in a blind alley.

Thus, even though religious discourse conceals, it also possesses the power to reveal. Just as there would be no revelation without a prior concealment, so, too, there would be no knowledge of the Reality without the instrument of religious discourse. For the purpose of communicating that which one already is, religious discourse is employed. And it is not as though religious discourse is something other than a part of ordinary, common everyday language. Religious discourse is part and parcel of ordinary language and what distinguishes it from the latter is merely the content and the purport. While ordinary language refers solely to the empirical world, religious discourse refers not only to the empirical world but also the Reality with name, form, and attributes (*saguṇa Brahman*) and to the Reality as one and non-dual (*nirguṇa Brahman*).

"The letter of the law killeth while the spirit of the law quickeneth."[38] Language was declared to be an instrument of ignorance as well as an instrument for liberation. As well, religious discourse was said to conceal as well as to reveal. At the epistemological level the two-level theory of religious discourse pertains. Its dichotomy and purpose must be clearly understood for no amount of objectification will ever give rise to an immediate knowledge of an "other."

The Advaitin maintains that religious discourse refers primarily and ultimately to that which is immediately evident and immanently present in the depth of each and every being. It refers to the Being of all beings. It seeks the irreducible substratum and source of all else. "It has all the necessity of a logical truth, with this difference that its necessity is not merely one that belongs to analytic propositions but one that is immediately and self-luminously felt to be real."[39]

SECOND-LEVEL PROBLEMS

Traditionally a question has been raised as to the propriety of interpreting certain religious discourse statements by an indicated meaning. Words in general are said to possess two powers. Either they denote a primary meaning which is their expressive power or else they denote a secondary meaning which is their indicative power. Only when the primary meaning is not applicable does one resort to the secondary meaning. The question has been raised as to whether the Advaitin violates the principle of the indicate meaning. An indicated meaning is necessarily connected to the primary meaning and if the Absolute is without any distinguishing characteristics, then there is no direct denotation of words which are applicable to it. And if the prior power of denotation cannot be exercised, then how can one evoke the word's indicative meaning or power?

Earlier it was revealed that a similar problem was raised in regards to analogy in the West. If God is God, then there doesn't seem to be any way in which to connect the two analogates. Since *Brahman* is not an objective entity having qualities, direct denotation seems impossible. Therefore such expressions as: *"Satyam, jñānam, anantam"* cannot denote their primary meanings and only their indicated meanings connected with the original meanings must be employed. And yet this avenue seems to be closed as well, for there is no way to connect the indicated meaning with a nonexistent primary meaning.

One way of countering this objection is to propose that expressions like *"satyam, jñānam, anantam"* and so forth, do directly denote the Absolute. This solution is linked with the theory of a first-level of language and flows from the purport of impartite expressions or identity statements.

Another answer is that there do exist cases in which words have no primary application and a secondary sense is still intelligible. There does not seem to be an inviolable law that the primary meaning is always possible. For instance, in the description of the qualitative differences of the sweetness of sugar, honey, candy, and so forth, a direct expression is impossible and only a secondary implication is available. Or again, the bliss that is experienced in deep sleep is expressed as: "I slept well." Such an expression is only a secondary implication since no primary designation by word is possible of this bliss. This bliss is not an object of ordinary everyday knowledge and thus the necessity of resorting to secondary implication.

Lastly, it may be said that this objection which has been raised by the critics of secondary implication fails to realize that even granting that the primary meaning of the words does not apply, still their charge that the rule of implied meaning has been violated, is fallacious. The primary meaning has been acknowledged and then set aside as incompatible because the Absolute is without attributes. The attributive terms are acknowledged as denoting the *saguṇa Brahman* while at the same time they are acknowledged as indicating the *nirguṇa Brahman*. That this manoeuvre robs secondary implication of certainty does not bother the Advaitin, for they never looked for certainty there in the first place. Interpretation by *lakṣaṇa* is a methodological move which serves as an intermediate instructional device and nothing more is claimed for it. Thus, the defects inherent in second-level language do not stymie the Advaitin like it does other protagonists.

As an "other," the Reality or God will always be a God of the gaps. According to the theists, God is the creator of the universe and distinct from his creation. The gap created by such a conception creates several difficult philosophical problems. This God is held to be the omniscient, omnipotent, omnipresent creator of everything that exists. This would imply that one is caught between the horns of a dilemma involving either pantheism or a denial of human freedom. It raises the question as to whether the finite conceptions of humanity can ever be adequately applied to this estranged God. If God is the Prime Mover, the First Cause, and thus within the causal scheme, does God leave the world entirely to the operation of the laws of nature or not? Out of what did God create the universe? Did this material exist outside himself? Did this original substance exist before creation, and if so, where and how? How to reconcile the omnipotence and benevolence of God with the inequalities of life without attributing incapacity or partiality to God? And even were it granted that these problems could be surmounted, what is the justification or grounds upon which one bases one's claim that anything actually exists corresponding to this God?

This gap between God and his creation is nonexistent for the Advaitin. The universe is not said to be created. It is but the way in which the Absolute appears under the limiting adjunct of ignorance. It is but an appearance (*vivarta*). Ordinarily two things are said to be causally related when one of them produces the other. The producer is called the "cause" and the produced is called the "effect." The cause is said to be different from the effect and anterior to it. However, Advaita, instead of maintaining that cause and effect are distinct, treats them as appearances of the same Reality. That is, it is not an identity between finite causes and effects in the world that is being maintained, but an identity between the world and the Absolute. The causal relation is thus neither a *de novo* creation nor a transformation, but merely an appearance. From the ultimate point of view, there is no such thing as one thing causing another. The universe cannot be logically said to be created. It is only the way in which the Absolute appears under conditions of space and time, as it were.

It is true that the Scripture seems to speak with two voices. There are passages characterizing God as the cause of the world and the ground of all auspicious qualities. However, this creationist position is countered by texts which declare non-duality. The Advaitin interprets the first type of statements figuratively and the latter ones literally; hence the two levels of language. Creation texts are said to be a methodological device to lead individuals from the familiar to the unfamiliar, from the known to the unknown. By employing the technique of prior superimposition and then subsequent denial, the non-dual Reality is gradually revealed. First qualities like omniscience, omnipotence, omnipresence, and causality are superimposed upon the Absolute and then, as these traits are revealed to contain irreconcilable difficulties upon a deeper analysis, they are subsequently negated. Thus, ultimately it is revealed that there is no causation and that the world is but an illusory appearance—even as the snake is an illusory appearance in the rope. The snake is not a real creation, but merely something which is nonexistent appearing as something existent. Like the causal relation between the substrate and what is superimposed upon it, the effect appears only so long as delusion appears. But for the substrate there would be no superimposed delusion. Past, present, and future, there is actually only the substrate appearing.

SATKĀRYAVĀDA AND ASATKĀRYAVĀDA

There are two traditional positions in regards to the cause-effect relation: Either the effect is preexistent in the cause (*satkāryavāda*) or else the effect is nonexistent in the cause prior to its production (*asatkāryavāda*). However, both positions are riddled with inconsistencies. The basic position of those who hold that the effect is a *de novo* creation from the cause is that if such were not the case, causation itself would be meaningless. If the effect is preexistent, then why does it need to be produced? Thus, the cause and effect must differ and the effect must be nonexistent before its production by the cause. But this position raises two fundamental problems. First, the cause and effect relation regarding the material cause is unsatisfactory. Nothing can come out of something unless it is already existent in that something. If such were not to be the case, then it would amount to disclaiming the need for a material cause for the production of an effect. And second, if the efficient cause is separate from the material cause, then this implies a limitation to God. God, being the efficient cause, would be bound to work upon material independent of him. Furthermore, he would be limited to creating only those forms which this given material would admit of.

Those who hold that the effect is preexistent in the cause counter the objection that if such were the case, then causation itself would be meaningless by saying that if the effect is not preexistent in the cause, then anything could come out of anything. There would be no determinative cause for a specific effect. Milk could come out of sand and then, only sometimes. In rebuttal, the opponents object that if the effect preexists in the cause, why does it need to be produced? The reply is that the effect is not in the cause as such; it is latent in the cause and has to be brought out. Thus, what is latent must become patient. Yet, still difficulties persist. Is the cause wholly transformed or only a part of it is in this process? If the whole cause is transformed, then the cause ceases to be, and what happens to the cause in which the effect is said to preexist? And if only a part of the cause changes into the effect, with the other part maintaining its substance, it will be like killing one-half of a hen to eat and trying to keep the other half to lay eggs with.

The reply to this is that what is meant in saying that the cause is transformed into the effect is that what was not previously manifested is now made manifest. The clay as cause does not disappear when the pot as effect is produced. What was the cause is now the effect, persisting in it.

Yet still the dialectics continues by asking exactly what this "manifestation" means? Again one is caught between the horns of a dilemma involving either the case that causation is redundant or else impossible.

Thus, it is that these two theories of causation destroy each other's position. If the effect is already existent, it is redundant to say that the already existent is created. And if the effect is nonexistent, it can never be produced. Either alternative fails to satisfy the demands of logic. Thus, it is that the Advaitin propounds the doctrine of non-origination.

According to the Advaita ontological position, the causal relationship cannot apply to the Absolute due to the fact of its being merest Being. Being is said to be the constitutive stuff of everything that is. It must not be thought of as the greatest common factor. As the constitutive reality of things it is the essence of all conscious and unconscious referents. As well, it is the source and ground of everything. Thus, it is the irreducible substratum, the most elementary, the simplest, the only non-composite. Merest Being cannot be one member in a causal series, even if that one be held to be the highest or the greatest. If it were a member of a series, then it would not be merest Being itself. Nor can merest Being be a product of evolution. For this would imply that the world came from non-being which is logically absurd. Non-being is not the cause of anything whatsoever precisely because it is nothing. Even to deny it and have the negation be real must mean that Being is embedded therein.

The provisional Advaita Vedānta theory of causation implies six requisites: (1) There is a relation in terms of succession in the cause-effect relationship. The cause is earlier and the effect is later. (2) The relationship between the cause and the effect is an irreversible relationship. The cause always precedes the effect and never vice versa. (3) The relationship between the cause and the effect is a necessary relationship and not a contingent one. (4) Cause and effect are not completely identical nor are they totally different. (If any two entities are absolutely different, they are not related by cause and effect, and if they are absolutely identical, then they are the same entity.) (5) The relationship between cause and effect is a one-sided relationship. The effect is always dependent upon the cause and not vice versa. (6) Between the cause and the effect, the cause alone is real.

This analysis will logically lead an individual to discover the impossibility of a causal scheme. From the seeming reality of the causal scheme at the empirical level, one is led to discover that philosophically speaking, there is no causation. By applying this criteria to the famous rope-snake example, the Advaita theory of causality will become clear.

The rope is the cause of the snake in the sense that the snake preexisted (so to speak) in the rope. It was sustained by the rope and finally disappeared back into the rope. All the time there was nothing else there than the rope. The rope never ceased being a rope, even while it appeared as the snake. This is the very essence of the idea, a thing appearing differently without ceasing to be itself even during the different appearance.

Because every effect has a cause, the Absolute is cosmologically said to be the cause of the Universe. This needs some elucidation. Whenever the Advaitin speaks of causation (*pariṇāmavāda*), it is with regards to God (*saguṇa Brahman* or *Īśvara*). Whenever the Advaitin speaks of appearance (*vivarta*), it is with regards to the Absolute (*nirguṇa Brahman*). Since the Absolute (*Brahman*) is the only Reality, and if we seek a cause for the world as we see it given in experience, we employ the language of cosmology and say, the Absolute alone, if anything, could be the cause of the world and not anything else.

Theologically, Advaita is aware of the theoretical difficulties of a mere theism. Thus, this is only a provisional acceptance purely as a methodological device later to be abandoned for a purer concept of non-duality. Accordingly, the Absolute is considered as the substrate (*adhiṣṭhāna*) of an illusory appearance of the world. The term used here is *"vivartopādāna"* rather than "cause."

If God is the creator of the world, the theists run into difficulty relating to the material out of which the world is fashioned and its subsequent implications with regards to the efficient cause or Creator. Was this material preexistent and independent of God? What is the material itself made of? Is it a part of God? Does all of God change or only a part of him if this material is somehow God? What is the relationship therein? Is the universe a *de novo* creation or a transformation of something preexistent?

Supposing there is a world and God is the cause of it, the following questions must be answered. Why does a non-creative God suddenly become creative? What is the purpose of God's creation? If there is something left for God to achieve, then his perfection has been compromised and if there is not, then creation must be redundant. God is infinite and creation is finite. What could an infinite God desire from a finite creation? Yet, as the *Brahmasūtrabhāṣya* asks, "If *Īśvara* has no purpose, then how do we explain creation?"[40]

One attempt to overcome this dilemma is to propound the theory that creation provides a place in which individuals may work out their past merits and demerits. However, the flaw in this theory is that past deeds themselves also require a place and time in which they were performed, ad infinitum. The solution is merely postponed, but not solved. And to postulate a beginningless creation is to silence one's critics, but not to explain the phenomena of creation.

Asatkāryavāda or *ārambhavāda* postulates an efficient cause (God) and a material cause (atoms) and the effect is said to be a new production from the cause. Yet the defects of this theory include limiting the creative powers of God. If God is forced to work with the atoms given, which are co-eternal and independent with God, then only those forms which the nature of the material admits of can be created. And what is the relationship between God and this material? If there is no relationship between them, then the two merely exist side by side, not affecting each other. Yet, at this does not explain creation, there must be some sort of relation. If there is a relation, then what affects one must affect the other. It is all very well for creation to undergo change, but it plays havoc to have to accept the fact that God as well must undergo change. To propound the relation as one of "identity in difference" will not alleviate the problem. How is it possible for a thing to undergo change and yet at the same time to remain the same? Such is a logical impossibility. If there is a connection between the two causal correlates, then either both sides are affected, or else they are not related at all. One cannot have it both ways. To maintain both change and identity in the same entity is to divide that entity itself.

The Sāṅkhya theory of *pariṇāmavāda* or *satkāryavāda* says that the effect preexists in the cause. Yet as we saw earlier, this has unwelcome consequences in regards to the transformation of the cause. Since Sāṅkhya denies the need for an efficient cause (God), the problems with God undergoing change do not affect their theory. But, at the same time, it is unthinkable for an insentient matter (*prakṛti*) to produce the world by itself. An intelligent agent seems a necessary presupposition for the creation of things having a design.

Advaita provisionally accepts the Sāṅkhya theory of *pariṇāmavāda*, but modifies it in that *māyā* is the material cause in association with God as its power. However, since difficulties eventually do present themselves, the entire conception of creation is held to be (in the final analysis) without any ultimate significance to the Advaitin. It does have practical implications, but is not logically defensible. Thus, for all practical theological purposes the world may be said to be an actual change of *māyā* as the power of God, but in the ultimate analysis, it is but an appearance of *Brahman.* In other words, the world is nonexistent in *Brahman.*

Thus, the theory of transformation (*pariṇāmavāda*) is held to be only provisionally correct. It is a preliminary teaching device to the theory of the appearance of *Brahman* as the world (*vivartavāda*). It is a concession and, as a theory of creation, it may be more plausible than others. But any creation theory is beset by certain fundamental difficulties which are inherent in the very idea of change. It is said within Advaita Vedānta that the creation-stories have not a metaphysical import but a metaphorical one. There is nothing absolutely to be gained by the knowledge of creation. It is the identity of the Self with *Brahman* that is the purport of the creation texts.

The real is the *nirguṇa Brahman.* Theologically speaking, this *nirguṇa Brahman* in association with *māyā* is called "*Īśvara* or *saguṇa Brahman.*" And it is this *saguṇa Brahman* that creates the world. But philosophically speaking, there is no causation at all.

It is only by assuming the existence of the world that its cause is sought for. Cause and effect are relative terms. Any event, which is the cause of another event, requires to be explained in terms of its own antecedent. Such a process leads to an *infinite regress.* To arbitrarily draw a line somewhere is to compromise with logical consistency. There is no reason to presuppose an uncaused cause after asserting that every event has a cause. If such were the case, what is to prevent one from postulating that each event was itself uncaused? And then where is the question of causality at all?

Unlike the creation texts, which are one type of second-level statements and which are figurative and indirect, first-level statements (even at the empirical level) are a linguistic device, a methodological tool which *directly* refer to the Absolute. They are used to point to that which transcends all opposites, is immanent in, and is the basis of all experience. They are literal expressions naming a fact. They point directly to the Reality by naming it and there their work ends. The mind is accustomed to think that they refer to that which lies outside the sphere of one's senses. And this is then translated into "what lies outside the bounds of experience." Yet, these statements speak about that which everyone is intimately familiar with even when they seemingly are speaking about something else. The first-level statements equate and identify the individual with the Absolute. These statements are indicators of information of the highest import and of immediate significance. In actuality, according to Advaita Vedānta, there is nothing else than what these statements refer to.

Utmost care should be taken not to interpret first-level statements as advocating an invisible being or entity behind the phenomena. Advaita's non-duality expresses the absence of difference of every kind. The purport of first-level statements is just to convey this knowledge. That which is, is all there is. To posit a being behind the scenes is to posit something over and above what is given. First-level statements point to what should be the most obvious fact of any experience. They affirm the pure experience which always is. In every reference to an individual's "I," the Reality is manifesting itself. Though the "I"'s total significance may not be exactly cognized or appreciated, no experience takes place without it. It is the content of this "I" which religious discourse refers to.

The key to understanding first-level statements lies in each individual. If a disagreement arises, it should not be thought to exist in what is given. Nor will the disagreement lie in what is not given. To draw from John Wisdom's parable, the disagreement in understanding, when one exists, is like a disagreement over whether that patch is a garden or a wilderness. The question is not over whether there exists an invisible gardener or not. To postulate an invisible gardener is to introduce an additional fact not originally given, while to ask if the garden is really a garden or whether it is a wilderness is consistent with the facts as they are given and introduces nothing which is unseen or above the garden's appearance. Thus, while everyone is familiar with their "I," differences may arise over its exact meaning and significance. The fact stands as given but some may see therein the Reality manifesting itself while others may see nothing but a selfish little ego or an accidental by-product thrown out in evolution by matter.

The problem is a problem about a fact and what the fact implies regarding the nature of Reality. The "I" or the self has been singled out for this analysis since all other understanding not only presupposes this self, but is dependent upon it. Second-level language presupposes that the things it identifies are different. First-level language states that the "two things" are really identical. They express the absence of another. They are not mere emotional or conceptual possibilities. They state a fact and this fact is self-existent. And that which is self-existent, which has being in itself and for itself, is complete and immutable.

ONE-LEVEL LANGUAGE—(ABSOLUTE LANGUAGE)

The real or final position of the Advaitin in regards to religious discourse is that there is one level of language and that all language directly points to the Absolute. From an empirical point of view, the Advaitin admits all kinds of distinctions. But from the Absolute point of view, all such conceptual concessions lose their significance. *Brahman* is all this—*"sarvam khalvidam brahma."*[41] This is not a mere assertion but an indubitable fact of experience as well.

"Ekam eva advitīyam"—Brahman is one only, without a second, points to the fact that any and every appearance must necessarily signify that Reality. Every concept must be an indicator of it. At the two-level theory of language, certain expressions are said to denote this better than others. Obviously all objects reveal being (*sat*) in one way or another. And the subject who recognizes these objects reveals not only being, but also consciousness (*cit*). Thus, those expressions which point to the nature of the Absolute by not only dispelling

doubts as to its nature but also by indicating the constitutive oneness therein are distinguished by degree and kind.

Yet, truly the Absolute is not an extra-empirical something. Every aspect of experience, both subjective and objective, reveal it. Though it is generally lost in the bewildering quantity of appearances, it is none the less irrepressible. For the liberated individual, there is naught but *Brahman*. *"Brahmasatyam, jaganmithyā, jīvobrahmaiva nā 'parah"*—*Brahman* is the final truth; the world is not real, and the individual is non-different from *Brahman*. Whatever is manifested, is the Absolute. Hence, there exists no differentiation of the knower, the object of knowledge, and the act of knowing. It is not the reality of the empirical universe that is negated, for its reality is the Absolute which always is, but it is the mistaken notion that the universe of name and form is real in itself, independent of the Reality that is being negated.

Perhaps it seems paradoxical to declare that all language directly indicates the Absolute and at the same time to declare that "all is one." The aim is to discover an element of unity within the seeming multiplicity of entities. And such is to be realized, experienced, and not just thought about or believed in. The Absolute is not an extra-cosmic entity sitting somewhere in a far-removed heaven, but that which is immediate and direct and given in experience as the innermost self of all. To the realized individual there is no longer any recognition of distinctions. From the perspective of the liberated individual or the perspective of an Absolute Language, all that is, is only the Absolute. The affirmation of the theist or the negation of the atheist, with respect to this existing fact, does not alter it at all. There is only the one, non-dual Absolute which is manifesting itself as it is. Ignorance expects to see something else and thus a false identity appears. But that does not mean that the Reality is not here and now, eternally the same. An individual steeped in ignorance declares that multiplicity abounds and that all words have their own distinct individual meanings. But to the liberated individual, the Self alone exists and is non-dual. It is not one in the sense of the sun or one moon. To perceive an object demands a perceiver. The idea of "one" is a correlative term within the empirical world. But the non-duality or oneness of the Absolute means a complete identity of subject and object. Upon the removal of nescience, the bewildering duality of empirical existence is automatically removed and the ever-present Reality self-luminously appears.

The Reality is an indubitable experience for the inmost consciousness of everyone. It is neither perceived by the senses nor comprehended by the mind. It is directly and immediately experienced without the instrumentation of the senses or the mind and does not depend upon any external authority for its proof. The empirical world is dependent upon the mind and the senses for its perception and is always colored by them. Thus, the empirical world is never directly or immediately perceived. It is only when the senses and the mind have become absolutely calm that the consciousness in an individual immediately and directly experiences that it is identical with the Absolute.

Language at the empirical or two-level theory admits of a hierarchical order. But Absolute Language admits of no such hierarchy. One may illusorily imagine that the knowledge which language conveys is the result of an interaction of the senses with their objects. Time, place, and other circumstantial factors seem to determine the meaning. But all that is happening is that the mind is taking on a mode which one mistakes for the Reality. Due to ignorance, the Reality, which is always manifesting itself, is not realized and whatever is manifested through the mental modes is mistaken for the Reality. Depending upon its purity or impurity, the mind reflects the Reality for better or worse. Yet the Reality is what it is all the time. It is not something to be attained (and thus not natural to oneself). That which is subject to time is not only attainable, but also can be lost. Thus, Absolute language is but a way of "perceiving" or "realizing" that the Reality is forever manifesting itself. When ignorance is destroyed, the manifestation becomes apparent.

Different names are associated with the varied mutiplicity which appears as the world. These names appear to distinguish one thing from another. But even as the same individual may be called: "father," or "husband," or "son," or "Devadatta," or "farmer," and so forth, so, too, the Absolute is called by many names.[42] The names change, but the constitutive Reality remains the same. Gold is distinguished by various names and forms like rings, bracelets, necklaces, and so forth. But even as the names and forms undergo change, the gold remains as it is. "And as, my dear, by knowing one nugget of gold all that is made of gold is known, the difference being only in a name arising from speech, but the truth being that all is gold."[43]

All the things of the empirical world are endowed with five characteristics: Existence (*asti*), cognizability (*bhāti*), attraction (*priyam*), name (*nāma*), and form (*rūpa*). The first three of these characteristics constitute the basis of everything whatsoever. What makes one thing appear different from another is its apparent name and form. The name is only a convention of speech, but there is actually no essential difference between one thing and another. The name exists only in one's mind and thus the Upaniṣadic dictim, "All this is verily *Brahman*."

Clay may take different forms in a potter's hands and thus become known as pots, cups, plates, and so forth. Really speaking they are all clay through and through though they are individually called by various names. Each is a form in which the same clay appears. Even so, the Absolute appears in different forms and is called by various names. To concentrate on the form makes one forget the basis. A potter is indifferent to the various manifestations and knows that each item is only clay. The objects are so many forms in which the Reality appears. The appearances are invested with a name and form but what abides is the Reality.

This is the bold declaration of Advaita Vedānta, namely, that whatever is, is nothing but the Absolute. The entire manifold universe is but *Brahman*. As *Brahman*, it always exists and never undergoes any change. To realize this is to realize that all words refer only to that Reality. "As (the *Vedas*) are devoted to one object (only), that is, the knowledge (of *Brahman*), (the wise) know that they (consist of) one sentence (only). The oneness of *Ātman* (and *Brahman*) should indeed be known through the understanding of the meaning of (this one) sentence."[44] Names and forms are like an illusion conjured up by a magician. When the real nature of the illusion is pointed out, what disappears is only the illusion which presented itself as something other than what it is. Being unsubstantial and unreal, the illusion's appearance and disappearance has no ability to affect the nature of the Reality. Once one has realized this, one never imagines the illusion to be real and yet one can still enjoy the performance.

The purpose of positing a two-level theory of language, like the distinction between *parā vidyā* and *aparā vidyā,* is a conventional device necessary for instructing an individual about the Absolute (*Brahman*). Śaṅkara is emphatic that the purport of all statements is the *Parabrahman* or Absolute. The two-level theory of language may be said to embody methodological expressions, though it is obvious that the first-level statements correspond to what we've called "Absolute language." The former is an approach from the side of ignorance while the latter is an approach from enlightenment. The statements are the same; the perspective in which they are approached differs.

Second-level language serves to give an initial understanding at some level of ignorance or other which otherwise may not be forthcoming. This is due to the fact that the problem is not so much what is said about the Absolute as that one is saying something at all. Since the Absolute is One and non-dual, any statement is a negation of the intent. Any formulation becomes a falsification of it. Yet, since language is grounded in *Brahman,* ultimately it is about *Brahman.* Language continues and is necessary as long as ignorance continues. But once ignorance is destroyed, only the One, non-dual *Brahman* remains and thus any language that is heard becomes only Absolute Language.[45]

Advaita Vedānta posits that there is nothing to discover but ourselves. Religious discourse is not primarily about God, or the world, so much as it is about individuals. The question is not one of reason *versus* revelation or objectivity *versus* subjectivity. To realize oneself is not a "thought." It is not a concept to "understand." "That *Brahman* is immediate and direct, the Self that is within all."[46] Religious discourse is describing but one fundamental fact of the Reality being all that there is.

LANGUAGE ABOUT THE ABSOLUTE

When one posits the Reality of an "other," an entire legion of difficulties arise. The history of the proofs for the existence of God and the theory of causality are ample testimony to this, as we have seen earlier. The doctrine of causation, like all other relations falling in the realm of ignorance, is found to be unintelligible. The origin of the world, whether a creation of God or a process of natural evolution, involves difficulties in both cases. Knowledge of an "other" must be hypothetical and conjectural and since it is something to be attained, it is also liable to be lost. Paul Tillich went to the extent of saying that atheism is the inevitable result of placing God apart as a stranger. All this we have seen. But there is a further consequence to be explored.

Usually it is held that an anthropomorphic God is comprehensible but inappropriate as an object of worship or religious belief. An anthropomorphic God usually denotes some sort of incredibly powerful physical being in the minds of its devotees. And a sort of "cosmic man" has a referent, but such a referent is philosophically and religiously unacceptable. Yet, a non-anthropomorphic God seems to be utterly incomprehensible. Who or what does religious discourse refer to? Does it refer to anything at all? A non-anthropomorphic Reality seems rift with obscure terms which no one understands nor can relate to. In order for one to understand what one is saying when they speak of God or the Reality, this referent must have some empirical anchorage which one *can* relate to.

Yet, strange as it may seem, it is my contention that a non-anthropomorphic Absolute is more consistent and logical and can be empirically anchored easier than a theistic deity. This is not a disparagement of a theistic deity, but merely a statement about consistency and coherence. It is true that the Judaic-Christian-Islamic God is thought to be a non-anthropomorphic infinite individual transcendent to the world. Yet, since this God is, in some way or other, conceived of as an "other," the above difficulties still arise. A theistic deity is spoken of as possessing all perfections. They are praised in innumerable ways. Yet, no one has been able to prove or demonstrate in any plausible sense of these terms, the existence of this "other." Flaws, inconsistencies, and contradictions mar the doctrines and traditions which have tried. Thus, God is *Deus Absconditus* and should be accepted humbly on faith.

The non-anthropomorphic Absolute is charged with being dry and barren, perplexing and unintelligible. Yet the Advaitin calls it the most empirical of all empirical entities. It is the most elementary, the further irreducible substratum. The causal relation does not apply to it nor is it the result of evolution. Being indeterminate and undetermined, yet it is. It is immediately given and directly experienced as one's own Self. One's own Self cannot be denied without self-contradiction. It is constitutive of everything and hence is a concrete immediacy. It is immediately felt and not transcendentally deduced, it is an accomplished fact. It must be presupposed for any proof regarding it.

Yet it is precisely here that the strangeness of the Advaitin's thesis appears. Difference and multiplicity are plainly perceived. The testimony of one's sense organs as well as every type of inferential reasoning declares that distinctions exist. It would appear that the Advaitin is going counter to facts when he seeks to eradicate this perceived diversity and established non-duality.

Suppose one were to grant for the sake of argument that plurality exists at the empirical level and that perception and inferential reasoning vouch for the reality of difference. Yet, perception and inferential reasoning are concerned with things empirical—as they understand the term empirical. They have nothing to do with the trans-empirical or the "radically empirical." Isn't it a baseless presupposition to presume that religious assertions about the trans-empirical need to be compatible with empirical observances? As Gareth Matthews said:

> This might be a reasonable demand if we had already established that, e.g. geometrical assertions have clear non-geometrical consequences, that physical assertions have clear non-physical consequences, that ethical assertions have clear non-ethical consequences, etc. But in the absence of any such established conclusions, (such a claim) appears to be discriminatory against theology.[47]

The Advaitin posits that there is no conflict between perception and religious discourse (*śruti*) because they are each valid in their own spheres.

This answer operates from the level of the empirical world. If the Advaitin is challenged that this answer does not establish or prove that non-duality is the Reality, but merely avoids the challenge, then the Advaitin advances a "critique of difference."

The seeds of this critique can be found in Gauḍapāda's doctrine of non-origination (*ajātivāda*).[48] Śaṅkara then took up the thread and elaborated it with numerous arguments relating to change and causality.[49] But it was with Maṇḍana Miśra that the "critique of difference" was developed into a full and independent refutation of the reality of difference.[50]

Merely because differences is perceived by the senses does not prove that difference is real. Everyone perceive the sun to be small, but inference contradicts this perception and in this case, one's perception is erroneous. To ascertain the Reality takes an acute analysis and the notion of difference fails to withstand such an analysis. Advaita admits the world-appearance as it appears, but it denies that it is the Reality. Since the world-appearance is contradicted at a later stage and ceases to exist, Advaita's dialectics of difference shows it to be an unsustainable notion.

Maṇḍana's argument, simply put, is that perception simply reveals an object. It does not, nor is it able to, distinguish one object from another.[51] And since difference presupposes distinction, if perception does not convey difference, the notion of difference being perceived is wrong. To support this claim Maṇḍana says that the idea of difference involves negation and that this negation must be preceded by an affirmation. Yet in perception, there are not two functions, that is, the revealing (affirmation) of an object and the differentiating of it from another object (negation).[52] Perception simply reveals an object and there its work ceases. If differentiation follows, it is not due to perception.

The entire Buddhist philosophy is based on distinctions. Difference is the very nature of everything and the very manifestation of an object involves differentiation from others. Maṇḍana criticizes this view and shows how it is logically untenable. The notion of difference involves a relation between at least two things which are different from each other. If this difference constitutes the nature of a thing and is non-different from it, then they will both be identical with their essence and thus identical with each other. Yet this is absurd—that two different things are identical. Or again, since difference is mutual nonexistence, if difference is the nature of an object, then its nature would be nonexistent and the object too would be nonexistent, which is a *reductio ad absurdum*.

The opponent may contend that difference is real and does not constitute the nature of an object. But this means the difference is a relation between two entities that differ. Yet this will land one in an *infinite regress*. Difference will require another difference to prove itself and that difference another, and so on.

To argue that difference can be inferred from successful activity is to involve the fallacy of begging the question (*petitio principii*). The differences among two or more objects which is to be proven should not be assumed in the process of the proof. One cannot assume that one can infer from different activities that there is a difference in objects. Difference is difference, whether in objects or in activities and thus it is incumbent upon an advocate of difference to prove difference without assuming it.

Likewise Maṇḍana criticizes arguments which seek to establish difference by invoking time, mutually opposed characteristics like happiness and misery, mutually opposed attributes like permanence and non-permanence, and order.[53] The assumption that difference is real is unwarranted and cannot be proven by perception. Nor can difference be known through non-cognition (*anupalabdhi*) as the Bhāṭṭa Mīmāṃsakas say.[54]Neither can it be perceived as the Naiyāyikas posit.[55]

According to Advaita Vedānta's theory of perception, objects are cognized in indeterminate perception (*nirvikalpa pratyakṣa*) a mere existence (*sattā*). This existence constitutes the nature of the objects. Thus, on one sene, objects are cognized as non-different from one another. Since existence is common to all objects, it is impossible to negate one object from another. What constitutes the difference that is perceived is due to ignorance, while the existence which runs through all objects renders them non-different from one another.

The nature of an object is known when its cognition comes through a valid means of knowledge (*pramāṇa*) and when this nature is in accord with reason.[56] Difference cannot fulfill these two conditions. Difference is perceived no doubt, but this cognition does not come from perception. Maṇḍana compares the cognition of difference to a cognition of a fire-brand-circle (*alātacakra*). Though there is no circle of fire, it appears to be so. Nor does one say that the circle of fire is real just because it is cognized. Thus, though difference is perceived, the difference among objects is illusory.

One need not become complicated and elaborate in regards to this problem. Any object which is cognized, is cognized as a "this." The specific character of an object may not be constant, but the "thisness" of an object is unalterably present. Differences are inconstant and may cause confusion, but the identity or sameness of objects is cognized in "existence" (*sattā*) and "thisness" alike, at all times, and thus is simple and direct and immediately valid.

Thus, by grounding the incomprehensible, unqualified Absolute within each one's own personal experience, it is more than a mere assertion or theoretical concept and is established as an indubitable fact of experience. Any abstraction is an escape from this fact. Though it is customary to regard the impersonal Absolute as an abstraction and a theistic deity as something concrete, an analysis tends to reveal that just the reverse is the case. Any "other" is removed and thus uncertain and partakes of degrees of murkiness, while identity is an experiential fact which cannot be doubted.

A little analysis may make this point even clearer. The Advaitin speaks of two aspects of the Absolute. One can identify an "existent-aspect" (*sattā-rūpa*) and an "Absolute-aspect" (*Brahman-rūpa*). Due to its general nature, existence is apprehended in every cognition. But the Absolute aspect is specific and thus not apprehended quite like existence is. Two examples will render this idea clearer. We have already seen that the theory of transformation (*pariṇāmavāda*) explains the cause-effect relation between clay and a pot. But the cause-effect relation between the Absolute and the world has to be explained in terms of appearance (*vivartavāda*). In the former case, the clay pot is apprehended. But in the theory of appearance, *Brahman*, as the cause, is not apprehended. Second, when one perceives a rope-snake, the general nature of "thisness" is always perceived while the specific nature is not. Perception will express itself in the statement, "this is a rope." The "this" refers to the rope. The "this" is general while the rope is specific. Even when one erroneously perceives a snake (instead of a rope), it is perceived as a "this" and the specific aspect of snakeness is later, sublated upon a correct apprehension of the object. The "thisness" is never sublated however. In a similar manner, in every cognition, the "existent-aspect" as "thisness" is invariably apprehended while the "Absolute-aspect" is not.

Thus, one may conclude that difference is untenable. One's day-to-day life relies on the idea of difference to function, but that does not establish the reality of difference. Difference is said to be experienced (*prasiddha*) but not to be validly established (*pramāṇa-siddha*). Day-to-day life is possible only by assuming difference, but likewise the idea of difference is possible only by assuming day-to-day life. The problem of mutual dependence arises. Instead of throwing up one's hands in despair, religious discourse offers one a solution of non-difference in which absolute peace is found.

The infinite is bliss . . . he who sees nothing else, hears nothing else, and knows nothing else, attains everything in every way. And on what is the infinite established? On its own greatness or not even on greatness.[57]

CHAPTER 8

Retrospective of Results

Religious discourse seems to be an attempt to speak about the Absolute, God, Truth, and similar enigmatic ideas. Our concern involves what can and what cannot be expressed in language. Religious discourse uses ordinary language of day-to-day discourse in an extraordinary way. This means that besides being a strange kind of language, it is also a problematical one.

Problem: What is being conveyed? Nietzsche said, God is dead, and Paul van Buren said, now even the *word* "God" is dead. The ineffable and trans-empirical are adequate objects of religious belief and devotion but they are out of sight and reach. The empirical, though within sight and reach is not an adequate object of religious belief.

Problem: How can the relational convey the non-relational? How can the empirical convey the non-empirical? If the words which are applied to the objects of religious discourse do not have the same meaning as when applied to the objects of ordinary mundane language, then the exact nature of those objects becomes very difficult to define. Either agnosticism or anthropomorphism seems the inevitable result.

Problem: What is the basis for religious discourse as a whole? Is it grounded in a metaphysical system? A revelation? A linguistic convention? An empirical experience? Irrational and non-sensical discourse?

Problem: What is the relationship of religious discourse with experience? Trans-empirical objects are unverifiable and unreliable in terms of sense-experience.

Chapter one, "introduction," began with an introduction to the perplexities of religious discourse. What does religious discourse mean and what function does it play? Is it possible to speak of the Absolute at all? This introduction led into the theme of Advaita (chapter two) which itself is the prologue and essence of Śaṅkara's solution to the problem of religious discourse.

Śaṅkara's solution is that religious discourse refers to that which is immediately evident and immanently present in all experience. This grounds religious discourse empirically and an analysis of experience only goes to confirm this claim. In fact, a thorough self-enquiry is what is prescribed. The key fact to be noted is that religious discourse is posited to concern individuals, here and now, an not a God, above and beyond.

Chapter five, "Methods and Perspective," analyses the methods employed by Advaita to convey the knowledge of the Absolute. The methods listed include: The method of prior superimposition and subsequent denial, the method of *via negativa*, the method of implication, the direct hearing of purportful Scripture, the use of etymology, and the method of silence.

Then the question of methodology and the relation of epistemology to metaphysics was examined. Advaita employs a thorough-going analysis of the subjective and objective approaches to Truth and invokes both epistemology and metaphysics therein.

The sections on *Brahman*-Ātman purported that the individual is not different from the Universal. Both from the side of objectification, relation, and conceptualization, as well as from the subjective side, an impartite Reality is an existent fact. Thus, *Ātman* is *Brahman* and the ground is laid for a complete answer to the problem of religious discourse from the perspective of Advaita.

Chapter six, "East and West," summarized the linguistic speculations of the various philosophical systems. It was with as well as against, this linguistic scaffolding that Advaita's theory of religious discourse developed. It grew especially out of the theory of words as knowledge (*śabda pramāṇa*).

By knowing a system's epistemological position, one should be able to construct its metaphysics and vice versa. Nowhere is this more apparent than in the radical consistency and coherence of Advaita Vedānta. Once one is given

Advaita's presuppositions, the rest logically follows. Whether it is in Advaita's metaphysics or in its epistemological position, its unique interpretation in regards to religious discourse can be extrapolated and exemplified.

Cognitive discourse revolves around the concept of verification and validity and the problem it had to face was what it was referring to and how. Non-cognitive discourse concerned itself with analytic talk about talk and its problems related to the function or use of religious discourse.

Be it noted, that approaches to other religious systems assume different presuppositions from those assumed by Advaita Vedānta. Thus, the purpose of this chapter was not so much to compare the two perspectives as to present differing attempts to solve the problem of religious discourse. Since it is a new paradigm that Advaita is proposing, different attempts give a wonderful springboard from which to elucidate.

Chapter seven, "Advaita's Solution," makes emplicit what has so far only been suggested. There seems to be two paradigmatic approaches to the problem of religious discourse. Either it refers to an "other" and the approach to this remote and foreign other is mediate, or else, it refers to the very constitutive being of anything whatsoever and as such is direct and self-evident. The former postulates a gap between the individual and the Absolute while the latter posits complete non-difference.

Most of the expositions one find on Advaita make it sound extremely abstract and highly impractical. Yet, again and again it is stressed that the primary concern of Advaita is to declare the non-difference between the individual and the Absolute. Advaita declares that religious discourse primarily concerns individuals, here and now, and not a God, above and beyond.

I am attempting to show that methodologically, Advaita's analysis commences with existence and culminates in essence, declaring that in fact the two are not different. Advaita declares that religious discourse refers to that which is immediately evident and present—unlike the general approach to an "other" which in one degree or another, searches elsewhere. The Advaitin maintains that Scripture plays a crucial role in achieving liberation. Yet, its implications are immanently practical and radically empirical, and not otherwise as is generally expounded.

A proposal was made that Advaita holds a two-level theory of language a well as an Absolute level of language. The purpose of this distinction was to logically explain religious statements from the perspective of ignorance as well as from the perspective of enlightenment. Śaṅkara is emphatic that the purport of all statements is the Absolute. The two-level theory is merely a conventional device embodying methodological expressions for instructing an individual about the Absolute. One could say that the exegesis depends on the perspective in which religious discourse is being approached.

Another proposal was made that within this two-level theory of language, there is a first level of language which is a literal expression directly naming the fact of the non-dual Absolute as well as a second level of language that is secondary, symbolic, and figurative. This proposal stemmed from various proponents of Advaita who have claimed that there is no necessity to resort to secondary implication to interpret the *mahāvākyas*.

A final proposal was made that it is more logically consistent to speak of an unqualified Absolute than of a qualified theistic deity. Basically this claim was proposed because the so-called incomprehensible Absolute was grounded within each individual's own personal experience, not as an object but self-luminously evident, not in a theoretical concept or abstract idea but in fact. Since the Absolute is an indubitable fact of experience, it is immanently practical.

COMMENT

Any proposed solution is just that, "a proposed solution." It is a common notion (and a mistaken one according to this thesis) that Advaita Vedānta is "dry and intellectual—abstract and impractical." It is my contention that the starting point of Advaita is concrete, here and now, and not a transcendent platform. Any philosophical system or religious tradition, once one's initial enthusiasm is aroused, is rapidly discovered to be tied to a specific tradition. And tradition means and entails precedence, solidarity, embodiment. Thus, no matter what the initial inclination may be, Advaita starts, not with a disembodied Absolute, but with the embodied individual, here and now. Definite implicit indicators of this approach include: *pañca koṣa viveka, avasthā traya vicāra,* and *sādhana catuṣṭaya* (subjective and objective approaches), as well as the explicit indicators which I have attempted to elucidate—the *mahāvākyas,* the implications of non-duality, and the purport of religious discourse.

NOTES

PREFACE

1. An explicit presentation of this solution is "new." Obviously the thought of Advaita Vedānta has existed for quite some time (at the very least for over 1,200 years, at the most it is as old as the *Vedas*). However, what is implied within Advaita's doctrine has never been explicitly stated vis-à-vis religious discourse.

2. What this "constitutive being" is and how it must be self-evident, immediate, and certain will be explained as we proceed.

3. Merely because one does not consciously know this does not make it any less so. Merely because one perceives a mirage in the desert does not imply that there is really water there. More of this later.

4. See John Hick's *Philosophy of Religion,* David Stewart's *Exploring the Philosophy of Religion,* or any of the many works about the Philosophy of Religion generally or Religious Language specifically.

5. Even if one is to grant the presuppositions of the various solutions proposed, they are still unsatisfactory. From Aquinas to Hick to today, the history of religious language is still looking for a viable presentation as to the nature and verification of religious statements.

6. Note: Alvin Plantinga's *The Ontological Argument* (1965); John Hick's *Arguments for the Existence of God* (1970); and Hans Kung's *Does God Exist* (1980)?

7. See P. T. Raju's *Structural Depths of Indian Thought, Preface.*

8. How few are the individuals who are even aware that virtually every modern University in India was founded by the British and thus has a syllabus which contains only Western philosophy. Thus, most Indian philosophers in the academic community are thoroughly trained in Western philosophy and many, if not most, also know Indian philosophy (learning the latter from pundits). Combine this fact with the epistemological, metaphysical, and ethi-

cal content which does exist within Indian philosophy, which such critics appear totally unaware of, it is no surprise the claims and charges which are advocated.

CHAPTER 1: INTRODUCTION

1. One sanskrit word for "world" is *"loka"*—which means a wide, open, extended, great space, or room to exist freely without hindrance and obstruction.

2. Obviously we are not talking about one's empirical self, but more of this later.

3. Note the importance given to linguistic analysis in the twentieth century.

4. Thus, atheism, agnosticism, Logical Positivism, and so on. Modern individuals have found themselves homeless; alienated from themselves, alienated from the world, alienated from others, and alienated from the Divine.

5. Advaita's declaration that "*Brahman* is real, the world in non-real and the individual and *Brahman* are not-different," which implies its doctrine of *māyā* renders Advaita's system unique in world thought.

6. Das Gupta, *History of Indian Philosophy*; Hacker, "Sankara der Yogin und Sankara der Advaitin" and "Beitrage zur Gelstes-geschichte Indiens."

7. S. Radhakrishnan and Chandradhar Sharma.

8. Radhakrishnan, S. Mudgal, and Ninian Smart.

9. N. Smart, *Doctrine and Argument in Indian Philosophy*, London, 1964, p. 104.

10. *Bṛhadāraṇyaka Upaniṣad* Bhāṣya Vārtika, I.iv.402.

11. I.e., Hick, Hare, Flew, and so forth.

12. This is not to deny that other systems *could* put forth a non-contradictory solution. I believe that a strong case could be make for a similar type of solution within the Ch'an/Zen school of Buddhism.

13. See pp. 25–26 of chapter 2. This thesis is presenting three significant assertions of which two are radically original.

14. I owe a debt to Professor Satchidananda Murty for the wording of this insight.

CHAPTER 2: ADVAITA AND RELIGIONS

1. Descartes' *Meditationes de prima philosophia* was an attempt to deal with the principles of human knowledge, with certainty and method.

2. *"Ayam ātma brahma"*—"the Self (*Ātman*) is the Absolute (*Brahman*).

3. The Cārvākas posited that the Self is the physical body; Sāṅkhya said that the Self is an eternal, immutable, conscious entity; Buddhism said the Self does not exist other than a cluster of factors.

4. Later we will take up an analysis of some systems in greater detail.

5. Y. B. Yeats

6. *Bhagavadgītābhāṣya* of Śaṅkara, XVIII.50. "Though quite self-evident, easily knowable, quite near and forming the very Self, *Brahman* appears to the unenlightened, to those whose understanding is carried away by the differentiated phenomena of names and forms created by ignorance, as unknown, difficult to know, very remote, as though he were a separate thing."

7. See R. A. Evans, *Intelligible and Responsible Talk about God.*

8. John Macquarrie, "The Logic of Religious and Theological Language," *Journal of Dharma,* vol. xvii, no 3 (July–Sept.) 1992, p. 171.

9. Ibid., p. 000.

10. Ibid., p. 172.

11. Note that, according to Advaita, qualifications pertain to the *vyāvahārika* realm and are spoken of *only* for (seeming) purification of the mind, not for achieving something.

12. *sādhana catuṣṭaya* or *nityanitya vastu viveka, iha amutra artha phala virāga, śama damādi sādhana sampatti,* and *mumukṣutva.*

13. *Bṛhadāraṇyaka Upaniṣad* IV.iv.22; *Vedāntaparibhāṣā VIII,* p. 211.

14. *Adhikāri* means both capable and entitled.

15. What this religious discourse is will be dealt with in Chapter 2.

16. Most Advaitins accept six sources of knowledge: perception, inference, comparison, presumption, non-cognition, and words as knowledge. I am indebted to Purusottama Bilimoria for the translation of *"śabda"* as "words as knowledge"; P. T. Raju translates *"śabda"* as "verbal knowledge" while many of the older Indian scholars used to translate it as "verbal testimony."

17. Religious discourse (*śabda pramāṇa*) is given a provisional status as a means of valid knowledge (which is not eventually sublatable). The final position of Advaita is that *Brahman* alone is real. This distinction will be made clear later.

18. A branch of one of the six orthodox schools of Indian philosophy. Its main objective was to establish the authority of the *Vedas* and to elucidate that the *Vedas'* main teaching is ritual.

19. *Bṛhadāraṇyaka Upaniṣad—asato mā sad gamaya.*

20. *Brahmasūtrabhāṣya* II.1.27. See also *B.S.B.* II.3.1.

21. *Bṛhadāraṇyaka Upaniṣad* Bhāṣya, Introduction.

CHAPTER 3: ADVAITA VEDĀNTA

1. **Āstika:** Nyāya, Vaiśeṣika, Saṅkhya, Yoga, Mīmāṃsā, and Vedānta, who all accept the authority of the *Veda* and **Nāstika:** Cārvāka, Jainism, and Buddhism, who all deny the authority of the *Veda*. Thus, in some sense or other, the *āstika* schools all accept *śruti* as a valid means of both empirical and trans-empirical knowledge while the *nāstika* schools do not.

2. Europeans first became acquainted with Advaita in the 1800s. There was a Latin treatise written by F. H. Windischmann (*Sancara sive de theologumenis Vedanticorum,* Bonn, 1833); G. C. Haughton's *The Exposition of the Vedānta Philosophy,* London, 1835; T. Foulkes' *The Elements of the Vedantic Philosophy,* Madras, 1860; and J. R. Ballantyne's *Christianity Contrasted with Hindu*

Philosophy, Madras, 1860. For Muller see, *Three Lectures on the Vedanta Philosophy*, London, 1984 and *The Six Systems of Indian Philosophy*, New Delhi, 1973. For Deussen see, *Das System des Vedānta*, Leipzig, 1883, *Vedānta und Platonismus im Lichte der Kantischen Philosophie*, Berlin, 1922, *The System of the Vedānta*, London, 1972, and *The Philosophy of the Vedānta*, Calcutta, 1957.

3. Setting the date of Śaṅkara's birth is one of the most controversial problems in the history of Indian philosophy. See Sengaku Mayeda's *A Thousand Teachings*, pp. 3–5.

4. Thibaut, *Vedānta Sūtras* with Śaṅkara's *Comm.*, p. xiv.

5. Natalia Isayeva, *Shankara and Indian Philosophy*, p. 17,

6. See such diverse scholarly opinions as those presented by Max Muller, B. Tilak, H. G. Jacobi, Sri Aurobindo, Thomas Hopkins, Norvin Hein, Swami Satprakashananda, P. T. Raju, Wilhelm Halbfas, and David Frawley to name but a few.

7. Swami Satprakasananda, *Methods of Knowledge* (Advaita Ashrama, Calcutta, 1974), pp. 307–308.

8. Indian tradition ascribes this collection and classification to him. That one individual really did such a work is open to doubt.

9. *Vedāntasara*, chapter 1.3, p., 2.

10. The *Vedas* are called *"śruti"* because they were "heard" by *ṛṣis*. They are said to be *apauruṣeya* because they are authorless, neither the divine nor human "composed" them. The *ṛṣis* merely transmitted the sounds which they heard.

11. *Mahābhārata, Bhīṣma parvā*, chapters 25–42.

12. *Brahma satyam, jagan mithyā, jīvobrahmaiva nā 'paraḥ*. This oft-quoted saying has no known scriptural location.

13. *Brahmasūtra* I.1.l.

14. *Māṇḍūkya Upaniṣad* II.7. *Ayam ātma brahma.*

15. Mayeda, pp. 11–12.

16. *Sajātīya, vijātīya, svagata.*

17. Actually the Advaitin admits of three levels of reality: the apparently real (*prātibhāsika*), the empirically real (*vyāvahārika*),

and the absolutely real (*pāramārthika*), but for our purposes here, the first two may be put together.

18. *Brahmasūtrabhāṣya* I.1.11.

19. *Chāndogya Upaniṣad* VI.2.1. *ekam eva advitīyam.*

20. Ibid., p. 000.

21. See *Vedāntaparibhāṣā*, p. 5.

22. *Bhagavadgītābhāṣya* of Śaṅkara, II.16. Also See *Brahmasūtra-bhāṣya* II.2.11 and III.2.4.

23. *Māṇḍūkyakārikā, IV.74.*

24. Bṛhadāraṇyaka Upaniṣad IV.3.22. *Yatra vedāḥ avedāḥ.*

25. Ibid., II.4.14.

26. See Radhakrishnan, *Indian Philosophy*, vol. II, p. 565. Also See R. Balasubramanian in *Perspectives of Theism and Absolutism in Indian Philosophy*, p. 48. The extensive scholarship over the philosophical differences between *"avidyā"* and *"māyā"* arose only after Śaṅkara's time.

27. Paul Hacker has voiced other ideas about the role of *māyā* in Advaita. This is not the place to take up his objections.

28. *Māṇḍūkyopaniṣad* with Gauḍapāda's *Kārikā* and Śaṅkara's *Commentary*, II.12, p. 97.

29. Ibid., III.19, p. 166.

30. Mahadevan, *The Philosophy of Advaita*, p. 79.

CHAPTER 4: ADVAITA VEDĀNTA PROSPECTUS

1. Bishop Durham suggested that the questions that concern us most, demand the oddest kind of language. See Ian Ramsey, *Religious Language* (London: SCM Press, 1957), p. 48.

2. "Genesis" 3.8. *The Holy Bible and Apocrypha*, Revised Standard Version (New York: Thomas Nelson and Sons LTD., 1959).

3. *Chāndogya Upaniṣad* VI.2.2. Tat aikṣata bahu syām prajāyeyeti.

4. The word *"aikṣata"* means literally "to see." It can be trans-

lated as: Saw, thought, desired. Its purport is to show that creation comes from a conscious source and not from an inert one.

5. *"Mathew"* 6.9. *The Holy Bible and Apocrypha.*

6. Arthur C. Danto, "Faith, Language, and Religious Experience," in *A Dialogue in Religious Experience and Truth*, ed. Sidney Hook (London: Oliver and Boyd, 1962), p. 147.

7. John Macquarrie, *God-Talk* (London: SCM Press, 1967), p. 34.

8. P. K. Sundaram, "Advaita and the Problem of Religious Language," *The Voice of Samanvaya,* 4 (March 1980),93.

9. See *Vedāntaparibhāṣā,* ch. 4. Compare with Aquinas' doctrine of analogical predication.

10. See Śaṅkara's commentary on the *Bṛhadāraṇyaka Upaniṣad* II.1.20. "Scripture does not speak about an unknown thing without having recourse to conventional words and their meanings."

11. "Whereof one cannot speak, thereof one must be silent." Wittgenstein, *Tractatus Logico-Philosophicus* 6.57.

12. Streng, Frederick J., *Emptiness: A Study in Religious Meaning* (New York: Abingdon Press, 1967), p. 105.

13. Augustine: *To Simplician: On Various Questions* 2.2.1.

14. *Brahmasūtrabhāṣya* II.2.17.

15. *Bṛhadāraṇyaka Upaniṣad* III.8.8.

16. See Murty, *Revelation and Reason in Advaita Vedānta,* p. 53.

17. Plato, *Timaeus 1,* in *The Dialogues of Plato,* trans. B. Jowett (New York: Random House, 1937), 2, p. 13.

18. *Kena Upaniṣad* 1.3–5.

19. Gustav Bergmann, *Logic and Reality* (Madison: University of Wisconsin Press, 1964), p. 177.

20. See P. K. Chakravarti, *The Linguistic Speculations of the Hindus* (Calcutta: University of Calcutta, 1933).

21. See Harold Coward, *The Sphoṭa Theory of Language* (Delhi: Motilal Banarsidass, 1980), p. 4.

22. *Vākyapadīya* 1.1.

23. *Vedāntaparibhāṣā* 1, p. 5.

24. *Brahma-satyam, jagan mithyā, jīvo brahmaiva nā 'paraḥ.*

25. The Great Sayings or Identity Statements specifically.

26. Advaita investigates and analyses not only the waking state of experience, but also the dream state and the deep sleep state as well as the "fourth" or turīya state.

27. *Māṇḍūkyakārikā* 2.203 in *Māṇḍūkyopaniṣad with* Gauḍapāda's *kārikā,* text and trans. Swami Nikhilananda (Mysore: Ramakrishna Ashrama, 1936). This is not to overlook the distinction Advaita makes between the *vyāvahārika* and *prātibhāsika.*

CHAPTER 5: METHODS AND PERSPECTIVES

1. Joachim Wach, *A Comparative Study of Religions*, ed. J. M. Kitagawa (New York: Columbia University Press, 1958).

2. Mircea Eliade, *Patterns in Comparative Religions,* trans. R. Sheed (London: Sheed and Ward, 1958).

3. Streng, *Emptiness: A Study in Religious Meaning.*

4. T. R. V. Murti, "Some Thoughts on the Indian Philosophy of Language." Presidential Address to the 37th Indian Philosophical Congress,1963.

5. *Brahmasūtra* I.1.4.

6. Ibid., I.1.1. *Athāto brahma jijñāsa.*

7. T. M. P. Mahadevan, *Invitation to Indian Philosophy* (New Delhi: Arnold-Heinemann Publishers (India) Private Limited, 1974), p. 379.

8. See Mahadevan, *The Philosophy of Advaita,* p. 57.

9. *Bṛhadāraṇyaka Upaniṣad* IV.5.15.

10. Ibid., I.4.10.

11. *Brahmasūtrabhāṣya* I.1.2. *Vastu yathātmyājñānam.*

12. *Vedāntaparibhāṣā* 1, p. 5.

13. Pañcadasī, text and trans. Swami Swahananda (Madras: Sri Ramakrishna Math, 1975) II.20–21. *"Sajātīya-vijātīya-svagata-bhedara-hitam."* See also Brahmasūtrabhāṣya II.1.14.

14. Compare: "Bertrand Russell, for instance in objecting that 'after all, Mr. Wittgenstein manages to say a good deal about what cannot be said' is clearly taking what can be said to be identical with what can be conveyed by means of language or what has meaning." Max Black, *Language and Philosophy,* (New York: Cornell University Press, 1949), p. 149.

1`5. *Bhagavadgītā* XIII.12.

16. *Brahmasūtrabhāṣya* I.i.4. *Svābhāvikapravṛttiviṣayavimukhīkaraṇārthānīti brūmaḥ.*

17. Bṛhadāraṇyaka Upaniṣad II.3.6.) Śaṅkara, commenting on this passage, says that the Absolute can never be properly denoted by any words—including the word "Absolute" (*Ātman*).

18. *Pratipādanaprakriyā* or *pratipādanaprakāra.*

19. *Naiṣkarmyasiddhi* III.103.

20. *Taittirīya Upaniṣad* II.1.1.

21. *Brahmasūtrabhāṣya* I.i.1.

22. *Dakṣināmūrti stotra* (Aesthetic Rapture), J. L. Masson and M. V. Patwardham (Poona: Deccan College, 1970), 2 vols.

23. *Brahmansūtrabhāṣya* I.1.4. "The work of the *śāstra* is to remove all distinctions to the self due to ignorance."

24. *Kena Upaniṣad* I.5.

25. Compare Wittgenstein: (1) early view: The structure of reality determines the structure of language, and)2) later view: Language determines one's view of reality.

26. His great contribution to epistemology was to shift the focus of one's attention from the objects known to the knower of the objects.

27. "Philosophers have always been concerned with method. Some, like Kant, have been very interested in it." Graham Bird,

Philosophical Tasks (London: Hutchinson University Library, 1972), p. 11.

28. Descartes, *Discourse on Method and Metaphysical Meditations*, trans. Walter Scott (London: Taylor and Francis, Ltd., 1952), p. 2.

29. "Analysis is emphasized in the methodology of metaphysics rather than cumulative evidence." (A. A. Vogel,*Reality, Reason, and Religion* (London: Longmans, Green and Company, 1959), p. 70.

30. Swami Satprakasananda, *Methods of Knowledge* (Calcutta: Advaita Ashrama, 1974), p. 63.

31. A. E. Taylor, *Elements of Metaphysics* (London: Metheun and Co., Ltd.), p. 4.

32. *Taittirīya Brāhmaṇa* VIII.8.5.

33. *Vākyapadīya* I.115.

34. *Tāṇḍya Mahā Brāhmaṇa* XX.14.2. This, (in the beginning), was only the Lord of the universe. His Word was with him. This Word was his second. He contemplated. He said: "I will deliver this Word so that she will produce and bring into being all this world."

35. Ṛgveda X.71.

36. P. K. Sundaram, "The Concept of the Religious Universal or the Sattā-Mahāsāmānya," *Voice of Samanvaya*, 5, No. 1 and 2 (Combined issue of April and October 1980), p. 43, n. 1.

37. *Māṇḍūkya Upaniṣad* II.7.

38. *Chāndogya Upaniṣad* VI.2.1.

39. *Māṇḍūkya Upaniṣad* II.7.

40. *Aitareya Upaniṣad* III.1.3.

41. *Māṇḍūkya Upaniṣad* II.7.

42. *Bṛhadāraṇyaka Upaniṣad* I.4.10.

43. *Chāndogya Upaniṣad* VI.8.7.

44. *Muṇḍaka Upaniṣad* III.1.7.

45. *Brahmasūtrabhāṣya* I.3.1.

46. Ibid., I.1.2.

47. Ibid., II.3.7.

48. Ibid., II.3.7.

49. Ibid., III.2.23.

50. See Śaṅkara's *bhāṣya* on Gauḍapāda's *Māṇḍūkyakārikā.*

51. Bṛhadāraṇyaka Upaniṣad III.8.8.

52. *Kaṭha Upaniṣad* I.3.15.

53. See *Taittirīya Upaniṣad Bhāṣya Vārtika* II.721.

54. P. K. Sundaram, *Advaita Epistemology* (Madras: University of Madras, 1968), p. 182.

55. G. W. P. Hegel, *Science ofLogic* (*Greater Logic*), trans. A. V. Miller (London: Allen and Unwin Ltd. 1969). 1.78.

56. F. H. Bradley, *Appearance and Reality* (London: Swan Sonnenschein and Co., Ltd., 1908), p. 30.

57. *Chāndogya Upaniṣad* Śaṅkara's *commentary*) VIII.1.1. and *Brahmasūtrabhāṣya* III.2.22.

58. *Bhāmatī* II.1.14.

59. See K. S. Murty's *Revelation and Reason in Advaita Vedānta*, p. 64.

60. *Pratyagātman.*

61. *Brahmasūtrabhāṣya* I.1.2—the cosmological proof. See Mayeda, p. 18ff.

62. *Bhagavadgītā* XIII.12.

63. *Brahmasūtrabhāṣya* III.2.22.

64. *Bṛhadāraṇyaka Upaniṣad* III.4.1.

65. *Chāndogya Upaniṣad* VI.2.1. *"Ekam evadvitīyam."*

66. *Pañcadaśī* II.20. *"Sajātīya vijātīya svagata bhedara hitam."*

67. *Brahmasūtrabhāṣya* IV.3.14.

68. *Aitareya Upaniṣad* III.1.3. *"Prajñānam brahma."*

69. *Taittirīya Upaniṣad* III.1.1.

70. *Kena Upaniṣad* II.3.

71. *Vedāntaparibhāṣā* I, p. 5.

72. *Brahmasūtrabhāṣya* I.1.1.

73. *Kaṭha Upaniṣad* II.2.15.

74. *Brahmasūtrabhāṣya* I.1.1.

75. Ibid., p. 000.

76. *Kena Upaniṣad* I.4

77. *Brahmasūtrabhāṣya* I.1.4.

78. *Bṛhadāraṇyaka Upaniṣad* IV.4.20.

79. Ibid., II.4.14.

80. *Kena Upaniṣad* II.3.

81. *Bṛhadāraṇyaka Upaniṣad* III.4.2.

82. Ibid., III.7.23. (He is never thought, but He is the thinker. He is the inner controller; he is your *ātman*).

83. See Mayeda, p. 27ff.

84. Ibid., IV.3.16.

85. Raimundo Panikkar, *The Vedic Experience* (Berkeley and Los Angeles: University of California Press, 1977), p. 13.

CHAPTER 6: EAST AND WEST

1. *Ṛgveda* 10.71; 5.10.2; 10.114.8; and *Bṛhadāraṇyaka Upaniṣad* IV.1.2.

2. See Hiriyanna, *Outlines of Indian Philosophy* (Bombay: Allen & Unwin [India] Private Ltd., 1978), p. 44.

3. Hiriyanna, *Essentials of Indian Philosophy* (Bombay: Blackie and Son Publishers Pvt. Ltd., 1978), p. 44.

4. See T. R. V. Murti, "Some Thoughts on the Indian Philosophy of Language." PresidentialAddress to the 37th Indian Philosophical Congress, 1963.

5. See *Ṛgveda* IV.58.3 wherein Speech is symbolized as the Bellowing Bull of great fecundity and the Great God who descends into the world of mortals.

6. Some Vaiśeṣikas (Kaṇāda) seem to treat verbal testimony as a valid source of knowledge while others (Praśastapāda) do not.

7. In Indian philosophy, this dichotomy is known as the distinction between *vidhi vākyas* and *artha vākyas*. In Western philosophy today, language is generally acknowledged to be many-dimensional and is said to have more gradations and uses than was once imagined. Thus, though there is a distinction made between "descriptive and prescriptive" language, or between "informative and emotive" language, the distinctions shouldn't be overemphasized.

8. See *Sarvadarśana Saṁgraha,* trans. E. B. Cowell and A. E. Gough (India: Cosmo Publications, 1976), p. 6.

9. A. J. Ayer, *Language, Truth, and Logic,* 2nd ed., (New York: Dover Publications, 1949), p. 35.

10. Ibid., p. 120.

11. A. J. Ayer, *The Revolution in Philosophy* (London: Macmillan and Co., 1956), p. 74.

12. Ludwig Wittgenstein, *Tractatus Logico-Philosophicus* 6.11, trans. D. F. Pears and B. F. McGuiness (London: Routledge and Kegan Paul, 1961).

13. See J. L. Evans, *The Foundations of Empiricism* (Cardiff: 1965).

14. A. J. Ayer, "Logical Positivism: A Debate," in *A Modern Introduction to Philosophy,* ed. A. Pap and Paul Edwards, rev. ed. (New York: Free Press, 1965), p. 743.

15. John Wisdom, *Philosophy and Psycho-analysis,* pp. 245–246.

16. Ibid., p. 50.

17. Aquinas held that God was wholly transcendent and perfect and thus human beings can at best know about God's existence, but not his essence.

18. F. C. Copleston, *Aquinas* (Harmondsworth: Penguin, 1955), pp. 126–127.

19. Anthony Flew, "Theology and Falsification," *New Essays in Philosophical Theology*, p. 96.

20. Ibid., p. 000.

21. Ibid., pp. 98–99.

22. A. MacIntyre, *New Essays in Philosophical Theology*, p. 202.

23. The opening words of Pascal's Memorial, dated November 23, 1654. See John Hick, *Philosophy of Religion*, p. 51.

24. H. J. Paton, *The Modern Predicament* (London: Allen and Unwin, 1955), p. 58.

25. *Arthasaṁgraha of Laugākṣi Bhāskara*, ed. and trans. D. V. Gokhale (Poona: Poona Oriental Series 18, 1932), p. 3.

26. *Mīmāṃsāsūtras* with Śabara *bhāṣya*, trans. Ganganatha Jha, Gaekwad's Oriental Series, vols. 66, 70, 73 (Baroda: Oriental Institute, 1933, 1934, 1936), I.1.2.

27. *Prakaraṇapañcikā*, ed. Mukunda Sastri (Banares: Chowkhambha Sanskrit Series 17, 1903), pp. 15–16.

28. *Mīmāṃsāsūtras* I.1.1. *Athāto dharma jijñāsa.*

29. Ibid., I.2.1. This refers to the well-known division of the *Veda* into *vidhi-vākya* (injunctions) and *artha-vākya* (existential passages).

30. *Ślokavārttika* of Kumārila Bhaṭṭa, trans. Ganganatha Jha (Calcutta: Asiatic Society of Bengal, 1909), 2.1.1.

31. See S. Radhakrishnan's *Indian Philosophy,* vol. 2, p. 389.

32. See the *Mīmāṃsāsūtras,* ch. 1.

33. For a modern interpretation and analysis of this "no author" idea, see Mohanty, "A Fragment of the Indian philosophical tradition—Theory of Pramāṇa," *Philosophy East and West*, vol. 38, no. 3, July, 1988, pp. 259–260 and Bilimoria, "On the Idea of Authorless Revelation (Apauruṣeya)," *Indian Philosophy of Religion,* Roy Parrett, ed., Dordrecht, 1989.

34. *Mīmāṃsāsūtras* I.1.27–32.

35. John Hick, *Philosophy of Religion* (New Delhi: Prentice-Hall of India, 1973), p. 75.

36. See *Faith and Logic: Oxford Essays in Philosophical Theology*, and *Philosophies of Religion.*

37. See *The Existence of God, Philosophy of Religion*, and *Faith and Knowledge: A Modern Introduction to the Problem of Religious Knowledge.*

38. See *An Analytical Philosophy of Religion.*

39. See *Religious Language: An Empirical Placing of Theological Phrases.*

40. See Price's *Belief.*

41. *Bhagavadgītābhāṣya* of Śaṅkara XVII. 66.

42. *Brahmasūtrabhāṣya* of Śaṅkara I.1.1.

43. See *Bhāṣāpariccheda* 164, wherein Nyāya-Vaiśeṣika distinguish two types of sounds: Inarticulate (*dhvani*) and articulate (*varṇa*).

44. The distinctive cause of *śābdipramā* is *śabdapramāṇa.*

45. *Vedāntaparibhāṣā* of Dharmarāja Adhvarindra, text and trans. Swami Madhavananda (Belur Math, Howrah: The Ramakrishna Mission Sarada Pitha, 1972), p. 86.

46. *Bṛhadāraṇyaka Upaniṣad* with the *commentary* of Śaṅkara, text and trans. Swami Madhvananda (Almora: Advaita Ashrama, 1975), 2.1.20, p. 214.

47. *Vedāntaparibhāṣā* IV, p. 110.

48. See S. Chatterjee, *The Nyāya Theory of Knowledge* (Calcutta: University of Calcutta, 1978), pp. 350–354.

49. William Pepperell Montague, *The Ways of Knowing* (London: Allen and Unwin, 1925), p. 39.

50. *Vedāntaparibhāṣā* IV, p. 150.

51. Ibid., 4, p. 116.

52. See *Brahmasūtrabhāṣya* of Śaṅkarācārya, text and trans.

Swami Gambhirananda (Calcutta: Advaita Ashrama, 1977), II.1.27, p. 355. Also see *Brahmasūtrabhāṣya* II.3.1; *Bṛhadāraṇyaka Upaniṣad* III.9.26; *Naiṣkarmyasiddhi* III.67; and *Taittirīya Upaniṣad* with the *commentaries* of Śankarācārya, Sureśvarācārya, and Vidyāraṇya, text and trans. Alladi Mahadeva Sastri (Madras: Samanta Books, 1980) III.1.3, p. 715.

53. *Tattvaśuddhi* of Jñānaghanapāda ed. S. S. Suryanarayana Sastri (Madras: Annals of Oriental Research, 1936), p. 11.

54. *Vedāntaparibhāṣā* IV, p. 98.

55. Ibid., IV, p. 102.

56. Ibid., IV, p. 107.

CHAPTER 7: ADVAITA'S SOLUTION

1. *Brahmasūtrabhāṣya* II.2.28.

2. H. P. Strapp, "S-Marix Interpretation of Quantum Theory," in *Physical Review*, vol. D 3 (March 15, 1971), pp. 1303–1320.

3. See *Exodus* 24.9–11 and *Exodus* 19.19.

4. See *I Kings* 18.39.

5. See D. S. Margoliouth, *Mohammed* (London: G. P. Putnam's Sons, 1923), p. 269.

6. *Vivekacūḍāmaṇi* 521.

7. *Brahmasūtrabhāṣya* II.1.4.

8. *Vedāntaparibhāṣā* I, p. 25.

9. St. Anselm's *Proslogian,* M. J. Charlesworth, trans. (Oxford: Clarendon Press, 1965), ch. 3.

10. Immanuel Kant, *Critique of Pure Reason,* trans. by Norman Kemp Smith (London: Macmillan and New York: St. Martian's Press, 1958), p. 505.

11. Tillich, *Systematic Theology,* vol. 1, p. 238.

12. *Bṛhadāraṇyaka Upaniṣad Bhāṣya* II.1.20.

13. Compare Meister Eckhart, "There is between God and the soul neither strangeness nor remoteness; therefore the soul is not only equal with God but it is the same that He is."

14. *Naiṣkarmyasiddhi* II.37.

15. "This view (that there is duality) is only for the sake of instruction. When the truth is known, all this duality is gone." Gauḍapāda's *Māṇḍūkyakārikā* I.80.

16. Waking, dream, deep-sleep, and the fourth levels; *vaikharī vāk, madhyamā vāk,* and *paśyanti vāk.*

17. *Mīmāṃsāsūtra* I.2.1-7 and *Brahmasūtrabhāṣya* III.4.36.

18. *Brahmasūtrabhāṣya* IV.3.14.

19. Ibid., p. 000.

20. *Brahmasūtrabhāṣya* IV.3.14.

21. Ibid., p. 000.

22. Ibid., p. 000.

23. *Bṛhadāraṇyaka Upaniṣad* II.4.14; IV.5.5.

24. *Brahmasūtrabhāṣya* IV.3.14.

25. Ibid., I.1.4 *Avidyākalpita bheda nivṛttiparatvat śāstrasya.*

26. "And being (already) released, he is released." *Kaṭha Upaniṣad* 5.1. "Being already *Brahman,* he attains *Brahman.*" *Bṛhadāraṇyaka Upaniṣad* IV.4.6.

27. *Naiṣkarmyasiddhi* III.103.

28. *Muṇḍaka Upaniṣad* III.2.9.

29. *Vedāntaparibhāṣā* VII, pp. 151–152.

30. See P. K. Sundaram, "Advaita and the Problem of Religious Language," *Voice of Samanvaya,* p. 98.

31. *Brahmasūtrabhāṣya* IV.1.3.

32. *Naiṣkarmyasiddhi* 2.54–56. *Pañcadasī* 8.46. *Bṛhadāraṇyaka Upaniṣad Bhāṣya Vārtika* I.1.4. Dharmarāja interprets the *mahāvākyas* literally. See *Vedāntaparibhāṣā.*

33. *Naiṣkarmyasiddhi* II.56.

34. *Pañcadasī* VIII.46.

35. *Iṣṭasiddhi* pp. 26–32.

36. *Taittirīya Upaniṣad* 2.9.

37. Attributed to Lao Tze.

38. P. K. Sundaram, "The Concept of the Religious Universal or the Sattā-Mahāsāmānya," *Voice of Samanvaya*, p. 38.

39. *Brahmasūtrabhāṣya* I.1.32.

40. Ibid., p. 000.

41. See also: *Muṇḍaka Upaniṣad* II.2.11. "Brahman alone is all this." *Chāndogya Upaniṣad* VI.2.1. "It is One alone, without a second." *Bṛhadāraṇyaka Upaniṣad* IV.4.19. "In *Brahman* there is no diversity whatsoever."

42. *Ekam sat viprābahudhā vadantī.*

43. *Chāndogya Upaniṣad* VI.1.6.

44. *Upadeśa Sāhasrī* I.17.9.

45. *Bṛhadāraṇyaka Upaniṣad* IV.3.22. *Vedāḥ avedāḥ.*

46. Ibid., III.4.1., and *Muṇḍaka Upaniṣad* III.2.9.

47. Gareth B. Matthews, "Theology and Natural Theology," *The Journal of Philosophy*, vol. lxi, no. 3 (30 January, 1964), 103.

48. See Gauḍapāda's *Kārikā* on the *Māṇḍūkyopaniṣad.*

49. See especially *Brahmasūtrabhāṣya* II.1.15–20.

50. See *Brahmasiddhi*. Padmapāda, Sureśvara, and other post-Śaṅkara Advaitins helped develop and contribute to this theme.

51. *Brahmasiddhi* part 1. *Āhurvidhātṛ pratyakṣaṁ na niṣeddhṛ vipaścitaḥ.*

52. Ibid., part 1, verse 3.

53. Ibid., part 1.

54. Ibid.

55. Ibid.

56. Ibid.

57. *Chāndogya Upaniṣad* VII.23.1.

BIBLIOGRAPHY

PRIMARY SOURCES

Advaitasiddhi of Madhūsudana Sarasvatī, trans. by Ganganatha Jha. Allahabad: 1914. Reprinted in Indian Thought Series 10.

Arthasaṁgraha of Laugākṣi Bhāskara, ed. and trans. by D. V. Gokhale. Poona: Poona Oriental Series 18, 1932.

Bhagavad Gītā, The, with the *Commentary* of Śri Śaṅkarācārya, trans. by Alladi Mahadeva Sastri. Madras: Samata Books, 1979.

Bhāmatī, The, trans. by S. S. Suryanarayana Sastri and Kunhan Raja. Madras: Theosophical Publishing House, 1933.

Bhāṣāpariccheda, with Siddhānta Muktāvalī, text and trans. by Swami Madhavananda. Calcutta: Advaita Ashrama, 1954.

Brahmasiddhi, ed. by S. Kuppuswami Sastri. Madras: Madras Government Oriental Manuscripts Series, no. 4, 1937.

Brahma Sūtra Bhāṣya of Śri Śaṅkarācārya, text and trans. by Swami Gambhirananda. Calcutta: Advaita Ashrama, 1977.

Bṛhadāraṇyaka Upaniṣad, The, with the *Commentary* of Śaṅkarācārya, , text and trans. by Swami Madhvananda. Almora: Advaita Ashrama, 1975.

Citsukhī, with Nayanaprasādiṇī, edited by Kashinath Shastri. Bombay: 1915.

Dakṣināmūrti Stotra, trans. by J. L. Masson and M. V. Patwardhan, 2 vols. Poona: Deccan College, 1970.

Iṣṭasiddhi of Vimuktātman, text and notes by P. K. Sundaram. Madras: Swadharma Swaarajya Sangha, 1980.

Khaṇḍanakhaṇḍakhādya, of Śrī Harṣa, ed. waith Anandapurna's *Khaṇḍanaphakkikavibhañjana* by L. S. Dravid Sastri. Chowkambha: Sanskrit Series 21. Benares, 1904-1914.

Māṇḍūkyopaniṣad, with Gauḍapāda's Kārikā and Śaṅkarācārya's Commentary, text and trans. and annotated by Swami Nikhilananda. Mysore: Sri Ramakrishna Ashrama, 1936.

Mīmāṃsā Sūtras, with Śabara *Bhāṣya,* trans. by Ganganatha Jha. Vols. 66, 70, 73. Baroda: Gaekwad's Oriental Series. Baroda Oriental Institute, 1933, 1934, 1936.

Naiṣkarmyasiddhi of Śri Sureśvara, trans. by S. S. Raghavachar. Mysore: University of Mysore, 1965.

Nyāya Kusumāñjali, with the Commentary of Haridāsa, text and trans. by G. B. Cowell. Calcutta: Baptist Mission Press, 1864.

Nyāya Sūtras with Bhāṣya and Vārttika, trans. by Ganganatha Jha, Poona: Oriental Book Agency, 1939.

Nyāya Vārttika Tātparyapariśuddhi, ed. with Vardamāna's *Prakāśa,* by V. P. Dvivedin and L. S. Dravid. Calcutta: Bibliotheca Indica 205, 1911–1925.

Nyāya Vārttika Tātparyaṭīkā, ed. by L. S. Dravid. Banares: Kasi Sanskrit Series 24, 1925–1926.

Padārthadharmasaṁgraha, with Śrīdhara's *Nyāyakandalī,* trans. by Ganganatha Jha. Benares: 1916.

Pañcadasī of Vidyāraṇya, text and trans. by Swami Swahananda. Madras: Ramakrishna Math, 1975.

Pañcapādikāvivaraṇa, ed. with extracts from Akhaṇḍānanda's *Tattvadīpana* and Nṛsimhāśrama's *Bhāvaprakāśikā,* by R. S. Bhagavatacharya. Vizianagram: Vizianagram Sanskrit Series 5, 1892.

Prakaraṇapañcikā, ed. by Mukunda Sastri. Benares: Chowkhamba Sanskrit Series 17, 1903.

Ṛgveda Saṁhita with Sayanna's Commentary, ed. by F. Max Muller. 4 vols. London: Oxford University Press, 1890.

Śabda Śakti Prakāśikā, ed. by G. C. Devasarma. Calcutta: 1918.

Sāṅkhya Sūtras of Kapila, with extracts from Vijñāna Bhikṣu's *Commentary,* trans. by J. R. Ballantyne. Calcutta: Asiatic Society.

Sarvadarśana Saṁgraha, trans. by G. B. Cowell and A. E. Gough. India: Cosmo Publications, 1976.

Śāstra Dīpikā with Yukti Snehaprapūrāṇī. Benares: Chowkhamba Sanskrit Series 43, 1916.

Ślokavārttika by Kumārilabhaṭṭa, trans. by Ganganatha Jha. Calcutta: Asiatic Society of Bengal, 1909.

Sphoṭasiddhi of Maṇḍana Miśra, trans. by K. A. S. Iyer. Poona: Deccan College, 1966.

Sphoṭavāda, ed. by V. V. Krishnamacharya. Madras: The Theosophical Society, 1946.

Taittirīya Upaniṣad, The, with the *Commentaries* of Śaṅkarācārya, Sureśvarācārya, and Vidyāraṇya, text and trans. by Alladi Mahadeva Sastri. Madras: Samata Books, 1980.

Tarka Saṁgraha, ed. with trans. and notes by S. Kuppuswami Sastri. Madras: 1951.

Tattvasaṁgraha Pañjika of Śāntarakṣita, with the *Commentary* of Kamalaśīla. Baroda: Government Oriental Series 30–31, 1926.

Tattvaśuddhi, ed. by S. S. Suryanarayana Sastri. Madras: Annals of Oriental Research, 1936.

Principal Upaniṣads, The, trans. by S. Radhakrishnan. London: Allen and Unwin Ltd., 1963.

Vaiśeṣika Sūtras of Kaṇāda, with comments from Śaṅkara Miśra's *Upaskāra* and Jayanārāyaṇa's *Vivṛti,* text and trans. by A. E. Gough. Banares: 1873.

Vākyapadīya of Bhartṛhari, with *Vṛtti* and *Paddhati* of Vṛṣabhadeva, ed. by K. A. Subramania Iyer. Poona: Deccan College, 1966.

Vedānta Paribhāṣa of Dharmarāja Adhvarin, text and trans. by Swami Madhvananda. Beur Math, Howrah: The Rama-krishna Mission Sarada Pitha, 1972.

Vivaraṇa Prameya Saṁgraha of Vidyāraṇya. Vizianagram Sanskrit Series 5, Banares, 1893.

Vivekacūḍāmaṇi, with text, notes, and trans. by Swami Madhavananda, Almora: Advaita Ashrama, 1921.

Yoga Sūtras of Patañjali, with *Yogasūtrabhāṣya* by Vyāsa and *Yogasūtrabhāṣyavivaraṇa* by Śaṅkara. Madras: Madras Government Oriental Series 94, 1952.

SECONDARY SOURCES:

Aquinas, Thomas. *Summa Theologica*. London: Eyre and Spottiswoode, 1963.

Ayer, A. J. *Language, Truth and Logic*. 2nd ed. New York: Dover Publications, 1949.

———. *The Revolution in Philosophy*. London: Macmillan and Co., 1956.

Balasubramanan, R. *Advaita Vedānta*. Madras: University of Madras, 1976.

Bergmann, Gustav. *Logic and Reality*. Madison: University of Wisconsin Press, 1964.

Bird, Graham. *Philosophical Tasks*. London: Hutchinson University Library, 1972.

Black, Max. *Language and Philosophy*. New York: Cornell University Press, 1949.

Bradley, F. H. *Appearance and Reality*. London: Swan Sonnenschein and Co. Ltd., 1908.

Braithwaite, R. B. *An Empiricist's View of the Nature of Religious Belief*. Cambridge: Cambridge University Press, 1955.

Carroll, Lewis. *Through the Looking Glass*. London: Macmillan, 1871.

Chakravarti, P. K. *The Linguistic Speculations of the Hindus*. Calcutta: University of Calcutta, 1933.

Charlesworth, M. J., trans. *St. Anselm's Proslogion*. Oxford: Clarendon Press, 1965.

Chatterjee, Satischandra. *The Nyāya Theory of Knowledge.* Calcutta: University of Calcutta, 1978.

Copleston, F. C. *Aquinas*. Harmondsworth: Penguin, 1955.

Coward, Harold. *The Sphoṭa Theory of Language.* Delhi: Motilal Banarsidass, 1980.

———. *Derrida and Indian Philosophy*. New York: SUNY, 1990.

Datta, D. M. *The Six Ways of Knowing.* Calcutta: University of Calcutta, 1972.

De Smet, Richard. "The Logical Structure of "Tattvamasi' According to Sureśvara's Naiṣkarmya Siddhi," *Philosophical Quarterly* (India), 33 (1961), pp. 255–265.

Descartes, Rene, *Discourse on Method and Metaphysical Meditations.* ed. J. F. Scott. London: Taylor and Francs, Ltd., 1952.

Deussen, Paul. *The System of the Vedānta,* trans. by Charles Johnson. LaSalle, Illinois: Open Court Publishing Co., 1912.

Deutsch, E. *Advaita Vedanta, A Philosophical Reconstruction,* Honolulu: University of Hawaii Press, 1973.

Devaraja, N. K. *An Introduction to Sankara's Theory of Knowledge.* Delhi: Motilal Banarsidass, 1962.

Evans, J. L. *The Foundations of Empiricism.* Cardiff: 1965.

Ferre, Frederick. *Language, Logic and God.* London: Eyre an Spottiswoode (Publishers) Ltd., 1962.

———, ed. "Analogy." *Encyclopedia of Philosophy,* vol. 1. London: Collier-Macmillan Limited, 1967.

Flew, Antony, ed. *Logic and Language*. First Series. Oxford: Basil Blackwell, 1951.

Flew, Antony, and MacIntyre, Alasdair, eds. *New Essays in Philosophical Theology*. London: SCM Press, 1957.

Granoff, P. *Philosophy and Argument in Late Vedānta. Śrī Harṣa's Khaṇḍanakhaṇḍakhādya*. Holland: Dordrecht, 1978.

Grimes, John. *Quest for Certainty: A Comparative Study of Heidegger and Śaṅkara*. Revisioning Philosophy Series. New York: Peter Lang Press, 1989.

———. *Sapta Vidha Anupapatti: The Seven Great Untenables— A Critical Study in Vedānta Dialectics*. Delhi, India: Motilal Banarsidass, 1990.

———. *The Naiṣkarmyasiddha of Sureśvara: A Monograph*. Sri Garib Dass Oriental Series, Sri Satguru Publications, Delhi, India, 1992.

———. "Advaita and Religious Language." *JICPR*. Vol. 6. No. 1. 1989.

———. "Two Paradigms of Religious Language." *Studies in Religion*. Vol. 19. No. 3, 1990.

Hacker, Paul. "Eigentumlichkeiten der Lehre und Terminologie Saṅkaras." *Zeitschrift der Deutschen Morgenlandischen Gesellschaft*. 100 (1950), pp. 246–286.

———. "Śaṅkarācārya and Śaṅkarabhagavatpāda. Preliminary remarks concerning the authorship problem." In *Kleine Schriften*. Edited by Lambert Schmithausen. Wiesbaden, 1978, pp. 41–58.

Halbfass, Wilhelm. *Tradition and Reflection: Explorations in Indian Thought*. New York: SUNY Press, 1991.

———. *India and Europe. An Essay in Understanding.* New York: SUNY Press, 1988.

———. *Studies in Kumarila and Sankara.* Studien zur Indologie und Iranistik, Monographie 9. Reinbeck. 1983.

Hegel, G. W. P. *Greater Logic (Science of Logic).* Trans. A. V. Miller. London: Allen and Unwin Ltd., 1969.

Hick, John, ed. *Classical and Contemporary Readings in the Philosophy of Religion.* Englewood Cliffs, N.J.: Prentice-Hall, Inc., 1964.

———. ed. *The Existence of God.* New York: Macmillan Co., 1964.

———. *Faith and Knowledge: A Modern Introduction to the Problem of Religious Knowledge.* Ithaca: Cornell University Press, 1957.

———. *Philosophy of Religion.* New Delhi: Prentice-Hall of India, 1973.

Hicks, George D. "Theory of Knowledge." *Encyclopedia Britannica.* Vol. 13. Chicago: W. Benton Publisher, 1948.

Hiriyanna, M. *Essentials of Indian Philosophy.* Bombay: Blackie and Son Publishers Pvt. Ltd., 1978.

———. *Outlines of Indian Philosophy.* Bombay: Allen and Unwin (India) Private Ltd., 1976.

Hobbes, Thomas. *English Works of Thomas Hobbes,* ed. W. Molesworth. London: Bohn: 1839–1840.

Holy Bible and Apocrypha, The. R. S. V. New York: Thomas Nelson and Sons, Ltd., 1959.

Hook, Sidney, ed. *Religious Experience and Truth*. London: Oliver and Boyd, 1962.

Hudson, W. D. "On Two Points Against Wittgensteinian Fideism," *Philosophy*, 1968.

Isayeva, Natalia. *Shankara and Indian Philosophy*. New York: SUNY Press, 1993

Jowett, B., trans. *The Dialogues of Plato*. New York: Random House, 1937.

Kant, Immanuel. *Critique of Pure Reason*. Trans. Norman Kemp Smith. London: Macmillan and New York: St. Martian's Press, 1958.

Kaviraj, Gopinath. "The Doctrine of Pratibhā in Indian Philosophy." *Annals of the Bhandarker Oriental Research Institute*. Poona: 1924.

Macquarrie, John. *God-Talk: An Examination of the Language and Logic of Theology*. London: SCM Press, 1967.

_____. "The Logic of Religious and Theological Language." *Journal of Dharma*. Vol. xvii. No. 3, July–Sept 1992.

Mahadevan, T. M. P. *Invitation to Indian Philosophy*. New Delhi: Arnold-Heinemann Publishers (India) Private Limited, 1974.

———. *The Philosophy of Advaita*. London: Arnold-Heinemann, 1876.

———. *Gauḍapāda: A Study in Early Advaita*. Madras, 1952.

Margoliouth, D. S. *Mohammed*. London: G. P. Putnam's Sons, 1923.

Mascall, E. L. *Existence and Analogy*. London: Longmanns, Green and Company, 1949.

Masson, J. L. and Patwardhan, M. V. *Aesthetic Rapture*. 2 vols. Poona: Deccan College, 1970.

Mayeda, S., *A Thousand Teachings*. New York: SUNY Press, 1992.

McTaggart, J. E. *Nature of Existence*. Cambridge: Cambridge University Press, 1988.

Miles, T. R. *Religion and the Scientific Outlook*. London: Allen and Unwin, 1959.

Mitchell, Basil, ed. *Faith and Logic*: Oxford Essays in Philosophical Theology. London: Allen and Unwin, 1957.

———. ed. *Philosophies of Religion*. London: Oxford University Press, 1971.

Montague, William Pepperell. *The Ways of Knowing*. London: Allen and Unwin, 1925.

Mudgal, S. *Advaita of Śaṅkara: A Reappraisal*. Delhi, 1975.

Murty, K. S. *Revelation and Reason in Advaita Vedānta*. Delhi: Motilal Banarsidass, 1974.

Nakamura, Hajime. *A History of Early Vedānta Philosophy*. Trans. by Trevor Leggett, Sengaku Mayeda, and others. Delhi, 1983.

Nielsen, Kai. "Wittgenstein Fideism," *Philosophy*. 17 July, 1967.

Panikkar, Raimundo. *The Vedic Experience*. Berkeley and Los Angeles: University of California Press, 1977.

Pap, A., and Edwards, P., eds. *A Modern Introduction to Philosophy*. Rev. ed. New York: Free Press, 1965.

Paton, H. J. *The Modern Predicament*. London: Allen and Unwin, 1955.

Phillips, D. Z. *The Concept of Prayer*. London: Routledge and Kegan Paul, 1965.

———, ed. *Religion and Understanding*. Oxford: Blackwell, 1967.

Plantinga, Alvin. *God and Other Minds*. Ithaca, N.Y.: Cornell University Press, 1967.

Potter, Karl. *Encyclopedia of Indian Philosophy: Advaita Vedānta up to Śaṅkara and His Pupils,* ed. by Karl H. Potter. Princeton, 1981.

Price, H. H. *Belief*. London: Allen and Unwin, 1969.

Radhakrishnan, S. *Indian Philosophy,* 2 vols, London: Allen and Unwin, 1951.

Raja, K. Kunjunni. *Indian Theories of Meaning*. Adyar: Adyar Library and Research Center, 1963.

Ramsey, Ian T. *Religious Discourse: An Empirical Placing of Theological Phrases*. London: SCM Press, 1957.

Randall, John H., Jr. *The Role of Knowledge in Western Religion*. Boston: Beacon Press, 1958.

Satprakasananda, Swami. *Methods of Knowledge*. Calcutta: Advaita Ashrama, 1974.

Smart, Ninian. *Doctrine and Argument in Indian Philosophy*. London, 1964.

Stapp, H. P. "S-Mastrix Interpretation of Quantum Theory." *Physical Review*. Vol. D 3, March 15, 1971.

Stcherbatsky, Th. *Buddhist Logic*. Vol. 2. Leningrad: Bibliotheca Buddhica 26, 1930.

Streng, Frederick J. *Emptiness: A Study in Religious Meaning*. New York: Abingdon Press, 1967.

Sundaram, P. K. *Advaita Epistemology*. Madras: University of Madras, 1968.

———. "Advaita and the Problem of Religious Language." *Voice of Samanvaya*. Vol 4, combined issue nos. 1 and 2, March 1980.

———. "The Concept of the Religious Universal or the Sattā-Mahāsāmānya." *Voice of Samanvaya*. Vol 5, combined issue of April and October, 1980.

Taylor, A. E. *Elements of Metaphysics*. London: Methuen and Co., Ltd.

Tillich, Paul. *Dynamics of Faith*. London: Allen and Unwin, 1957.

———. *Shaking of the Foundations*. Great Britain: Penguin Books, 1949.

———. *Systematic Theology*. London: Allen and Unwin, 1957, 3 vols.

Vogel, Arthur Anton. *Reality, Reason and Religion*. Longon: Longmans, Green and Company, 1959.

Wisdom, John. *Philosophy and Psycho-Analysis*. Oxford: Basil Blackwell, 1969.

Wittgenstein, L. *Tractatus Logico-Philosophicus.* Trans. by D. F. Pears and B. F. McGuiness. London: Routledge and Kegan Paul, 1961.

———. *Philosophical Investigations*. In German and English. Oxford: Blackwell, 1953.

Zuurdeeg, W. F. *An Analytical Philosophy of Religion.* Nashville: Abingdon Press, 1958.

INDEX